Bluegrass Banjo Breaks & Licks

BY FRED SOKOLOW

With Editorial Assistance
by Ronny S. Schiff

The Recording

Banjo, Other Instruments and Vocals: Fred Sokolow

Sound Engineer: Michael Monagan

Recorded and Mixed at Sossity Sound

PLAYBACK+
Speed • Pitch • Balance • Loop

To access audio visit:
www.halleonard.com/mylibrary

Enter Code
2325-3532-8922-9524

ISBN 978-1-5400-1218-0

Visit Hal Leonard Online at
www.halleonard.com

Contact us:
Hal Leonard
7777 West Bluemound Road
Milwaukee, WI 53213
Email: info@halleonard.com

In Europe, contact:
Hal Leonard Europe Limited
42 Wigmore Street
Marylebone, London, W1U 2RN
Email: info@halleonardeurope.com

In Australia, contact:
Hal Leonard Australia Pty. Ltd.
4 Lentara Court
Cheltenham, Victoria, 3192 Australia
Email: info@halleonard.com.au

CONTENTS

SONG LIST

INTRODUCTION

If you're a banjo player who's been bitten by the bluegrass bug, you need help! Bluegrass banjo is often played at blistering speed, and it involves instant improvisation. There's no simple pattern to learn and repeat; rather, there are dozens of patterns and licks you need to master—to play accompaniment *and* to solo.

This book is a compendium of essential three-finger banjo licks, bluegrass clichés, and backup and soloing tips. It shows you how to play intros, endings, and everything in between. You'll learn runs that go from one chord to another, how to vamp on a chord for as many bars as necessary, and how to approach a solo up or down the neck—in any key!

Bluegrass banjo is an ensemble style, and when you play with other people, you spend more time playing accompaniment than playing solos. That's why so much of this book is about backup licks to play during the vocals or when other instruments are soloing. Sometimes bluegrass banjo backup is just as interesting as the solos.

Along the way, you'll learn some bluegrass standards that serve as examples, showing you how to apply the licks you're learning. All the licks and tunes are played on sound files that you can access online. Make sure to listen to each track before trying to read the tablature or music notation—that's how to pick up on the rhythmic nuances that make all the difference.

Instant ad-libbing is an essential bluegrass skill. You can memorize a hundred classic bluegrass banjo solos—and that's part of being a bluegrass banjo player. But unless you know how to improvise, when you're called upon to play a song you haven't memorized, you're back to square one! However, once you've assimilated the material in this book, you're well on your way to playing and improvising bluegrass banjo… for real.

Good Luck,

Fred Sokolow

Fred Sokolow

Special acknowledgment must be made to Earl Scruggs, the founder of bluegrass banjo. There were other three-finger banjo pickers before him, but every bluegrass banjoist owes Scruggs a debt. So many of the licks and songs we all play came out of this one man's imagination. Copying him is still the best way to start learning the style.

About the Audio

To access the accompanying audio for download or streaming, simply visit *www.halleonard.com/mylibrary* and enter the code shown on page 1 of this book. The audio tracks are mixed so that the banjo is on one side of your stereo and the guitar and voice are on the other side. The PLAYBACK+ audio player allows you to pan left or right, slow down the audio without changing pitch, set loop points, and change keys!

The songs in this book are folk standards that have been performed and recorded by countless bluegrass artists. In case you're unfamiliar with any of them, listen to tracks 106–119. The licks and breaks (solos) in the book will make more sense if you know how each song sounds. The recorded tracks have a verse and chorus of each tune. You'll also hear classic bluegrass banjo backup licks throughout!

Note that when shorter licks or phrases are written with repeat bars, each one is played through three times on the accompanying audio track.

PRELIMINARIES

Fingerpicks

Though it's called "three-finger picking," bluegrass banjoists actually pick with two fingers and the thumb. Metal or plastic picks are always worn; they make you sound louder and give you that bright, hard-as-nails tone. The two fingers that are not in use—the ring and little fingers—rest on the banjo head, to brace the picking hand.

How to Wear Picks   Bracing the Picking Hand

Tuning

Though Earl Scruggs and other first-generation bluegrass pickers like Ralph Stanley and Don Reno sometimes played in C tuning and open D tuning, G tuning always was, and is, the main, standard bluegrass banjo tuning. It's an open G chord: if you strum the unfretted banjo strings in this tuning, you're playing a G major chord: gDGBD, or:

 Tuning

Track 1

     5 = G
     4 = D
     3 = G
     2 = B
     1 = D

Chords

Here are some common banjo chord shapes, both **open-position chords** (on the first four or five frets, using open strings) and **moveable chords** (that can be played all over the fretboard).

The fifth string is not included in grids throughout this book, unless it is fretted. Most of the time it is played unfretted; that's why it's often called a "drone string": the fifth-string note keeps ringing out over chord changes, giving the 5-string banjo a unique sound.

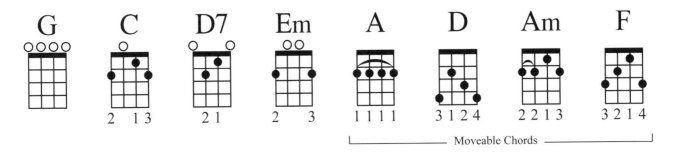

G   C   D7   Em   A   D   Am   F

        2   1 3   2 1   2   3   1 1 1 1   3 1 2 4   2 2 1 3   3 2 1 4

Moveable Chords

The Basic Rolls

Bluegrass banjo is based on seven types of rolls. When playing solos or backup, you don't repeat one roll over and over—*you mix them constantly*, going from one to another seamlessly. Still, the best way to learn each roll is to repeat it for several minutes, staying in rhythm and increasing your speed as you go.

Here are the basic rolls and several variations of each one. (There are countless possible variations, but these are the most often played.) Listen to each one carefully before playing it.

*Note that every example in this book is played with a **shuffle feel**, which means the eighth notes aren't played straight, but with more of a "bouncy" rhythmic feel. It's a very common sound throughout many musical genres, including blues, jazz, and bluegrass. Listen to the audio tracks to get a sense of it.*

 In and Out Roll and Variations

Track 2

If you're also a guitar player, this roll may be familiar. It's sometimes called "double thumbing."

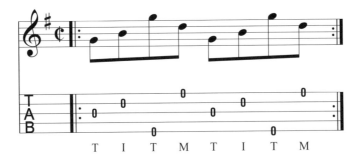

T   I   T   M   T   I   T   M

In the second variation on the next page, you slide on the third string from 2nd fret to the 4th fret, and pick the open second string just as the third string is arriving at the 4th fret. So, the slide and the picked second string are simultaneous.

A similar thing happens in the third variation with a pull-off lick. Fret the third string at the 2nd fret with your index finger and at the 3rd fret with your middle finger. Then you pick the third string and pull-off from the 3rd to the 2nd fret. You pick the open second string just as the pull-off is happening.

Many of these variations include "blue notes," which are not in the major scale. They add a bluesy flavor to bluegrass banjo. The flatted 3rd, flatted 7th, and flatted 5th are blue notes. The third string/3rd fret is a "blue note" (Bb, a flatted 3rd) in the key of G. So is the second string/2nd fret; it's Db, a flatted 5th.

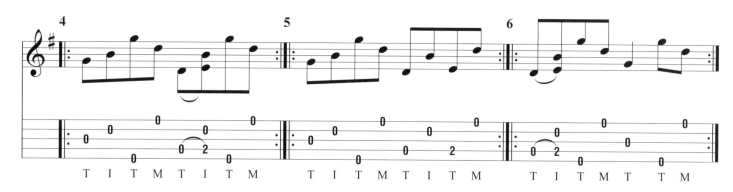

Forward Roll and Variations

Track 3

Any roll that goes from lower to higher strings (2-1-5, 3-2-1, etc.) is a "forward roll."

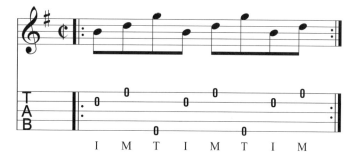

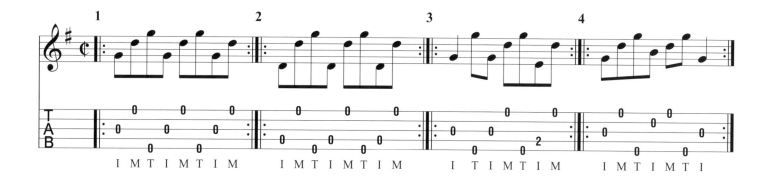

9

Double Index Roll and Variations

Track 4

This is sometimes called the "Foggy Mountain Breakdown roll," since it's played at the beginning of Scruggs' iconic instrumental. Notice that the third note can be picked with the index finger or the thumb.

The third variation is the lick used in "Foggy Mountain Breakdown." The second string hammer-on is simultaneous with the picked, open first string. In the fourth variation, the pull-off on the third string is simultaneous with the picked, open first string.

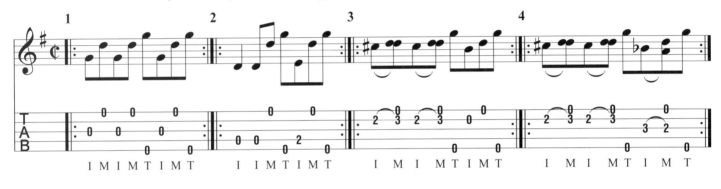

 Backward Roll and Variations

Track 5

If it goes from higher to lower strings (1-2-3, 1-2-5), it's a "backward roll." This roll is useful when the melody is on the first string.

10

Track 6

Forward/Backward Roll and Variations

T I M T M I T M

Listen to the rhythm of the triplet (three eighth notes played with the time value of two eighth notes) in Variation 3.

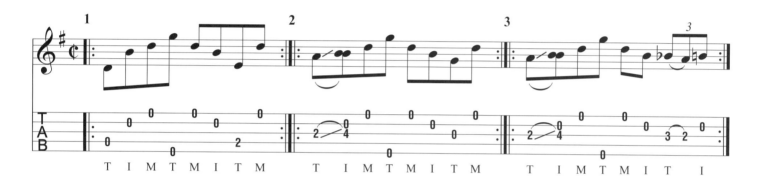

T I M T M I T M   T I M T M I T M   T I M T M I T I   I

Track 7

Double Backward Roll and Variations

Like the backward roll, this is useful when the melody is on the first string.

M I M T M I M T

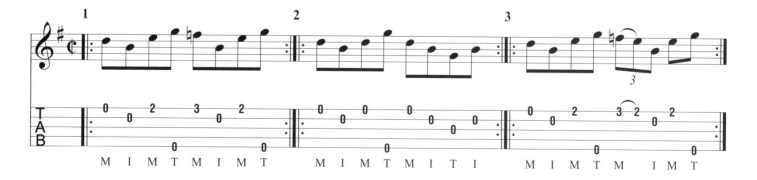

M I M T M I M T   M I M T M I T I   M I M T M   I M T

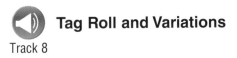
So named because it's used in tag endings, this roll is also used in backup and solos, just like the other rolls.

A Little Music Theory—The Numbers System

Throughout this book, you'll find references to the 1 chord, or the 4 or 5 chords. The language of music is often expressed with numbers rather than letters. Musicians say, "Go to the 4 chord," or "Go to the 2 minor." The numbers refer to the major scale steps. Since C is the first note in the C major scale, a C chord is the 1 chord in the key of C. Therefore, D, or D7 or Dm is the 2 chord; E is the 3 chord, and so on. In the key of D, E is the 2 chord.

No matter which key you're in, going from the 1 chord to the 5 chord has a certain sound, as does going from 1 to 4. It's the spaces between chords—the intervals—that give a chord progression its unique sound. Once you can recognize the sounds of the various intervals (1 to 4, 1 to 5), you understand how music works, and you can play a song in any key. You're not just memorizing letter names; you're feeling and hearing the song's structure.

Chord Families

Regardless of a song's key, the 1, 4, and 5 chords are the "usual suspects"—the chords that are most likely to occur. Countless bluegrass songs consist of just those three chords. They can be in any order imaginable. It's helpful to have the chord families memorized, especially in the most commonly used keys:

Key	1	4	5
C	C	F	G
G	G	C	D
D	D	G	A
A	A	D	E
E	E	A	B

Playing in All the Keys

By using a capo and/or moveable chords, all banjo licks can be played in any key! Here's how:

There are three types of licks in this book:

1. **G Licks:** played in open position (on the first four or five frets, using open strings)—they're useful when playing in the key of G.

2. **C Licks:** also played in open position—useful when playing in the key of C.

3. **Moveable Licks:** based on moveable chord formations—since these licks (and the chord shapes on which they're based) include no open strings, they can be played *anywhere* on the fretboard and are useful for all keys.

G licks are not exclusively useful for the key of G. You can use them in the keys of A♭, A, B♭, B, C, or D.

- **Key of A:** Bluegrass banjo players usually play in A by capoing up two frets and tuning the fifth string up to A. Then they pretend the capo is the nut, and use all of their G licks. The open G chord is now an A chord, open C is now D, and so on. All the G licks are now A licks. *This is where thinking in terms of numbers comes in handy: wherever you put the capo, the open chord is still the 1 chord, the C shape is still the 4 chord, and so on.*

- **Key of B:** Capo up four frets and tune the fifth string up to B. Now the open chord is B, the C-shaped chord is E, and so on. You can use all your G licks.

- **Key of B♭:** The same as B, only a fret lower and the fifth string is tuned to B♭.

- **Key of A♭:** The same as A, only a fret lower, with the fifth string tuned to A♭.

- **Key of C:** You can play in the key of C without a capo, using open-position chords. You can also capo up five frets, tune the fifth string up to C, and use all of your G licks.

- **Key of D:** The same as C, above, only two frets higher (tune the fifth string all the way up to D. Look into fifth string spikes—ask your local music store about them). It may make you sound like you're playing the Chipmunk's banjo, but it is sometimes done.

C licks are often used in the keys of D, D♭, E, E♭, and F, by using a capo and retuning the fifth string:

- **Key of D:** Capo up two frets, tune the fifth string up to A, and act as if you're in the key of C, using your C licks.

- **Key of D♭:** The same as the key of D, but one fret lower (capo and fifth string).

- **Key of E:** Capo up four frets and tune the fifth string up to B. The C chord is now E, and you can use all of your C licks.

- **Key of E♭:** The same as the key of E, but one fret lower (capo and fifth string).

Moveable licks can be used in any key. Earl Scruggs and subsequent bluegrass pickers often played in the keys of D, E, and F, sans capo. This method saves you the hassle of reaching for and applying a capo in the middle of a performance, and it has another advantage—you don't lose the banjo's low notes.

- **Key of D:** Tune the fifth string up to A and play a D formation for your 1 chord, with the fourth string left open or fretted. The open G is your 4 chord and the barred A is your 5 chord, though there are moveable alternatives.

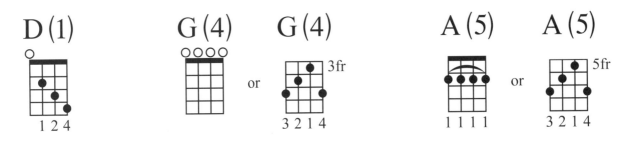

- **Key of E:** Tune the fifth string to G♯ or B. Use open-position chords as well as moveable chords.

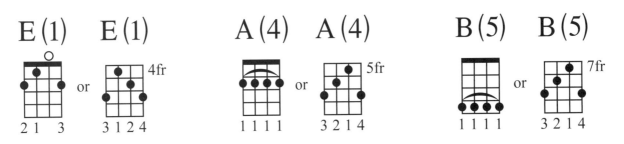

- **Key of F:** Tune the fifth string up to A, and use open-position or moveable chords.

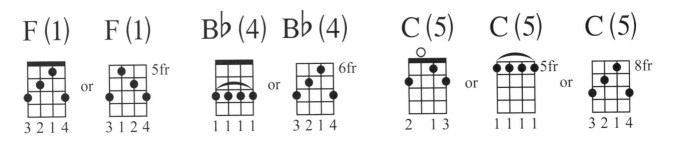

As you can see, there are two ways to play in the keys of F, C, or E (with or without a capo), and three ways to play in the key of D (two different capo positions or no capo). It's good to have alternatives! Each approach offers a slightly different sound.

ACCOMPANIMENT (BACKUP) LICKS

The Endless Forward Roll—An Easy Accompaniment Method

A simple way to get started playing accompaniment is the "endless forward roll" method.

Endless Forward Roll

Track 9

- Play a forward roll that doesn't repeat after eight beats, but keeps rolling. Start with the index finger on the third or second string:

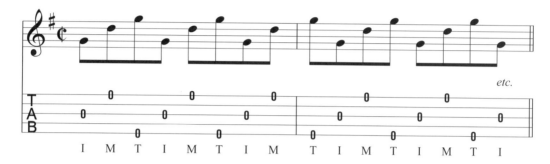

- Make the chord changes and keep rolling. You can stop the roll before a chord change and start up again on the new chord. For example, here are two bars of G followed by two bars of C:

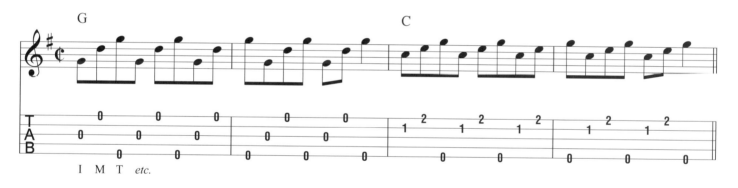

- To break the monotony of the constant forward roll, you can stop and start anytime you like. You can also add "pinches" on the first and fifth strings whenever you feel like stopping to get your footing. *("Pinch" means: play the first and fifth strings simultaneously with your thumb and middle finger.)*

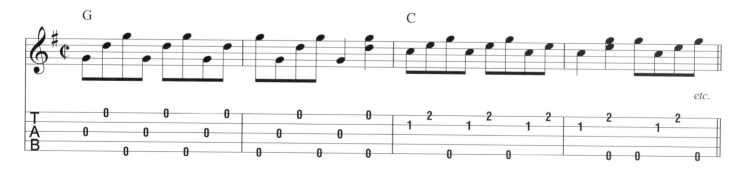

Here's a popular bluegrass work song with a typical three-chord progression: G–C–G–D–G. Many bluegrass songs share this chord sequence: 1–4–1–5–1. The endless forward roll is interrupted and started over when the chords change:

"Nine Pound Hammer"—Endless Forward Roll in G

Tag Endings

If you play the endless forward roll, change chords at the right time, and end a verse or chorus with a tag ending, then you'll sound like a bluegrass banjo player! Here's a classic tag ending; it's similar to the second variation of the tag roll (Track 8):

Tag Endings and "Nine Pound Hammer" (Last Few Bars in G)

Here's the tag in context, at the end of a verse:

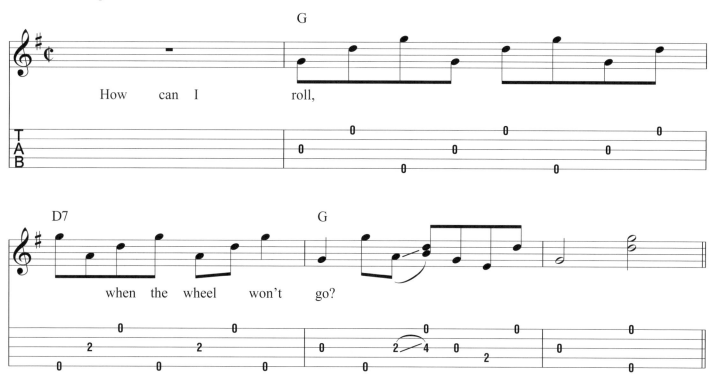

Here are some more tag endings:

Tag Endings in G

Track 12

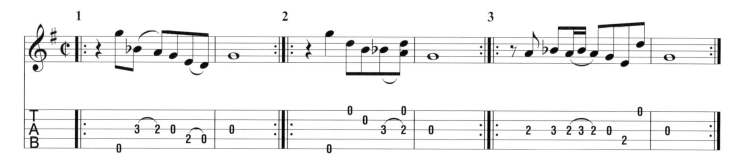

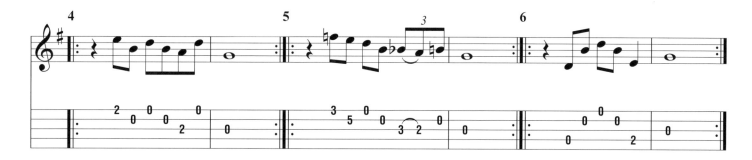

Tag Endings in C

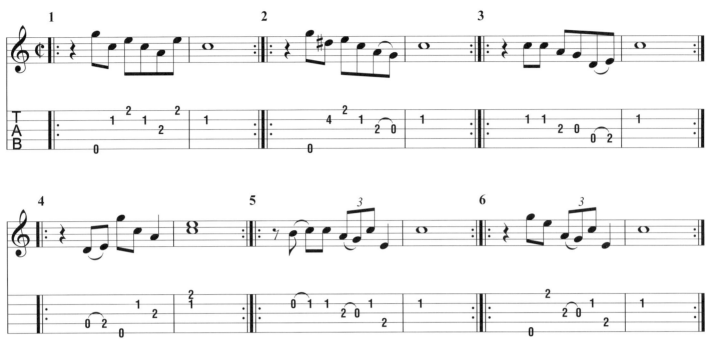

Moveable Tag Endings

Moveable chords are chord shapes that include no open strings. Since all the strings are fretted in these chords (except for the fifth/drone string), they can be played all over the fretboard. For example, the barred A chord can move up or down to create many chords:

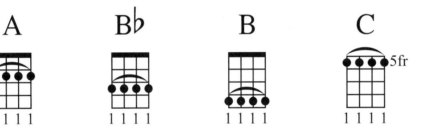

Tag endings and other licks can be based on moveable chords. Here are four moveable shapes to use for tag endings. They can be played in any key, as illustrated by the following examples.

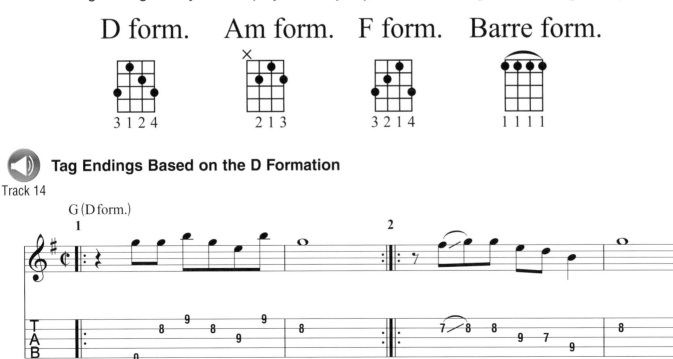

Tag Endings Based on the D Formation

G (D form.)

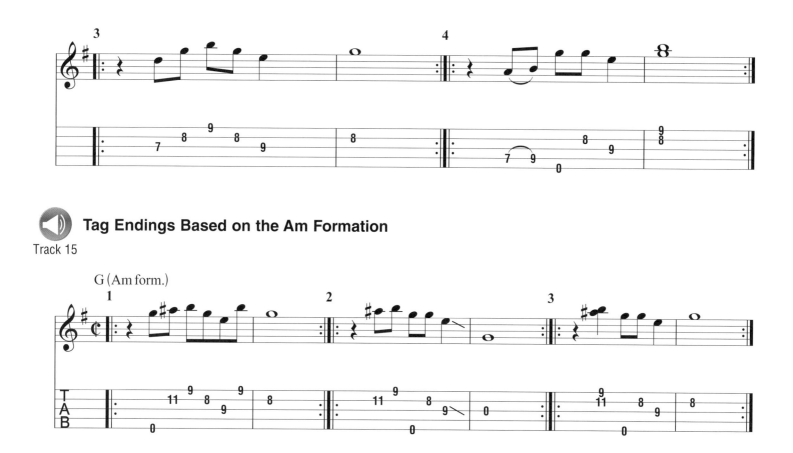

Tag Endings Based on the Am Formation

Track 15

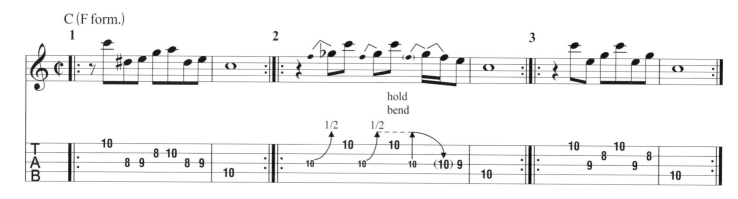

The second lick of Track 16 involves **bending** (also called "choking," or "stretching") the third string. Fret the third string with your ring finger, pick it, and push the string up across the fretboard (towards the fourth string) to create the effect heard on the track.

Tag Endings Based on the F Formation

Track 16

C (F form.)

Tag Endings Based on the Barre Formation

Track 17

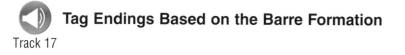

Connecting Licks—Open Position

Connecting licks lead from one chord to another. Bluegrass guitarists play **bass runs**. Here's the banjo equivalent:

Connecting Licks for G and D

Track 18

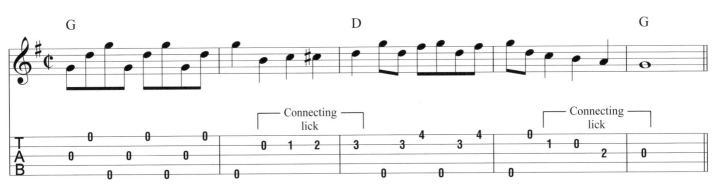

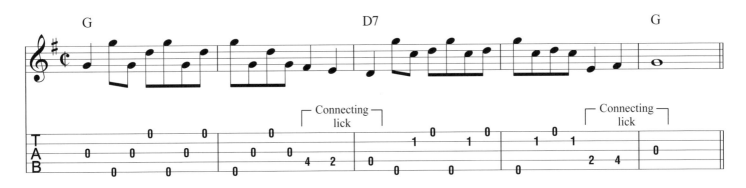

"Little Birdie" is an old, two-chord mountain song. It makes use of some connecting licks.

"Little Birdie"—in G

Track 19

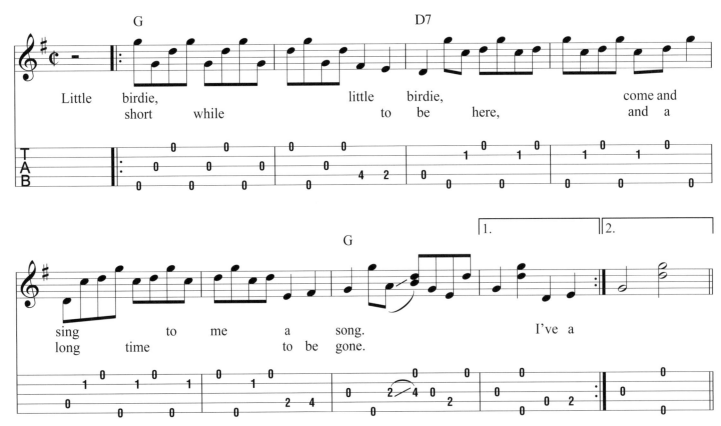

20

Here are some licks connecting C to G, and G to C:

Track 20

Connecting Licks for G and C

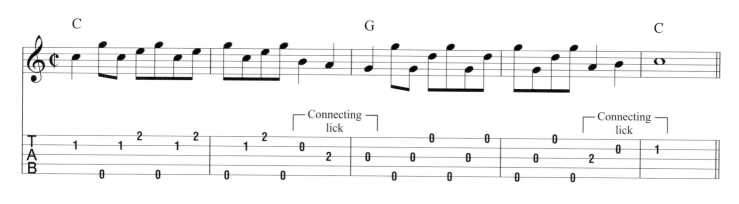

Play "Little Birdie" in the key of C, using connecting licks.

Track 21

"Little Birdie"—in C

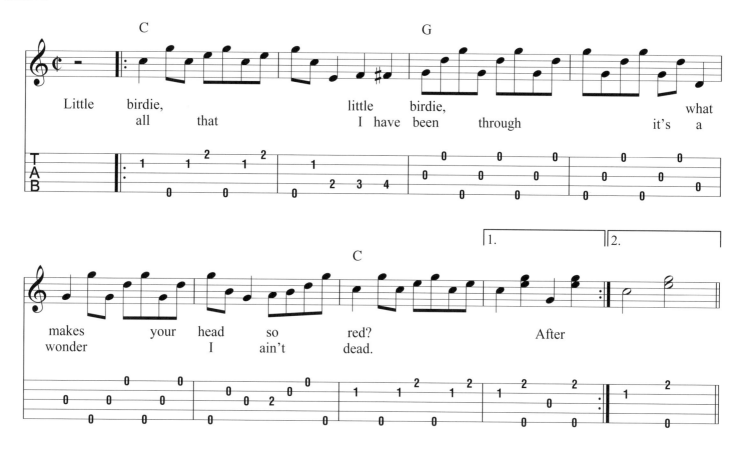

Now that you know connecting licks that go back and forth from G to C and G to D, you can play three-chord songs in the key of G that include those licks. Add a tag ending, and you'll start sounding like a bluegrass banjo player! Here's an old folk song popularized by the Carter Family, "Bury Me Beneath the Willow," with those components. It has a chord progression that is common to many bluegrass tunes:

1 | 1 | 4 | 4 | 1 | 1 | 5 | 5 | 1 | 1 | 4 | 4 | 1 | 5 | 1 | 1 |

"Bury Me Beneath the Willow"—in G (with Connecting Licks)

Track 22

To play backup for a three-chord song in the key of C, you need connecting licks from C to F and back:

Connecting Licks for C and F

Track 23

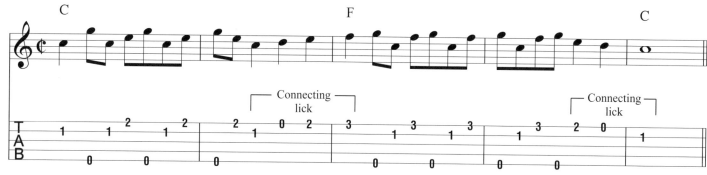

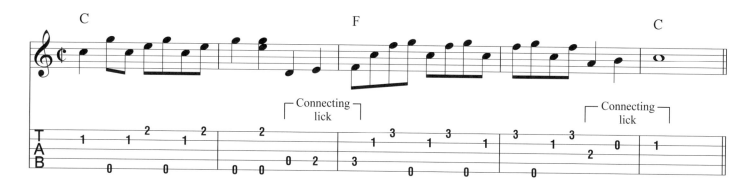

Track 24 — "Bury Me Beneath the Willow"—in C (with Connecting Licks)

Moveable Connecting Licks

These licks connect moveable chords: F and D formations and the barre shape.

Track 25 — Connecting Licks for D and F Formation

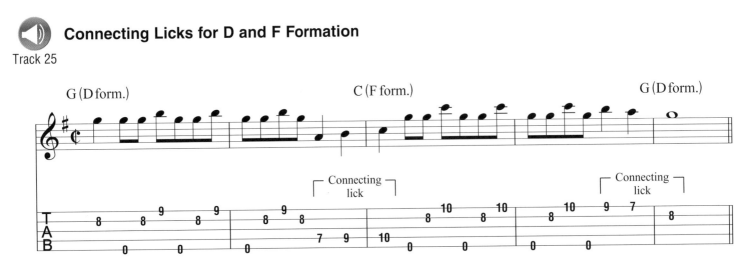

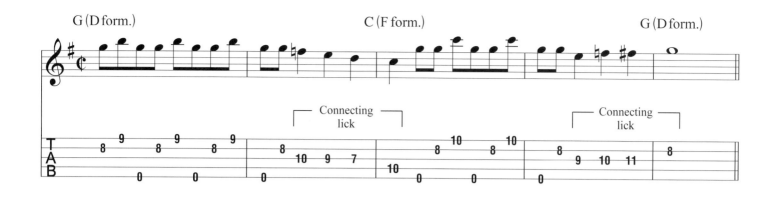

Connecting Licks for F and Barre Formation
Track 26

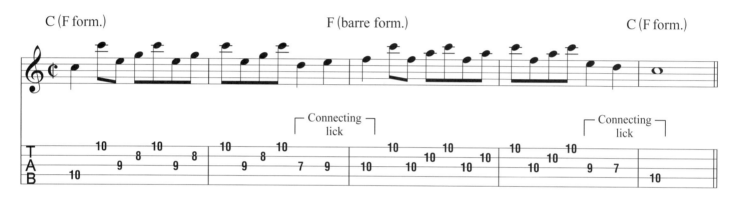

Connecting Licks for Barre and D Formation
Track 27

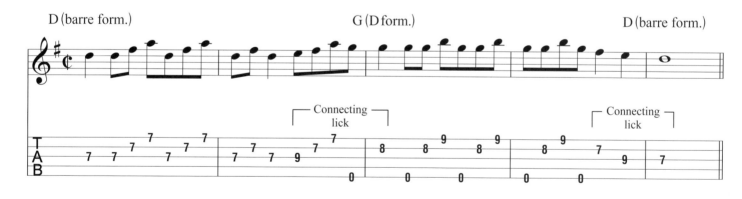

25

Track 28

"Bury Me Beneath the Willow" (with Moveable Connecting Licks)

Pedaling Licks

When you hang on one chord for several measures, constant forward rolls can become monotonous. There are many other rolls and licks to play that can make your backup interesting, even though you're staying in one place (as opposed to moving from one chord to another). Like pedaling on an exercise bicycle, there's the feeling of movement even though you're not going anywhere! Here are some sample licks that work over different chords. They are one- or two-bar licks, so if you have more than two bars to play, you can randomly mix any of the licks. (Repeating one lick over and over is boring; they are repeated on Track 29 for practice purposes only.)

Pedaling G Licks

Track 29

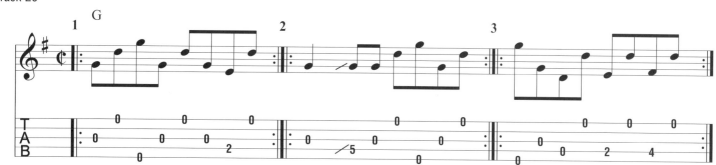

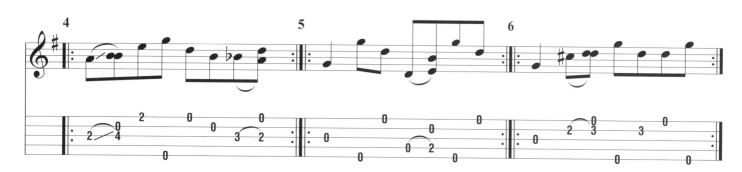

Pedaling C Licks

Track 30

Pedaling D and D7 Licks

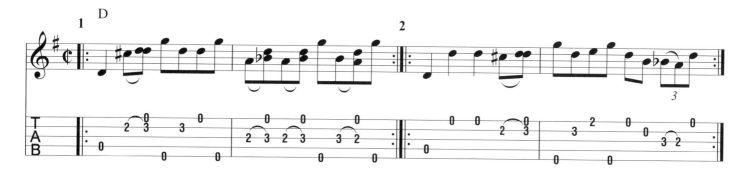

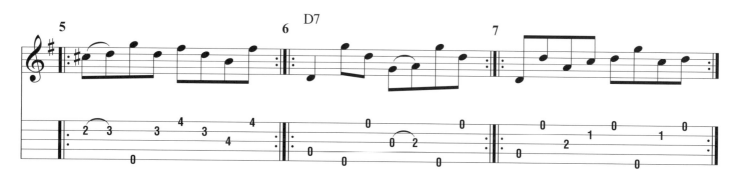

Here's a verse of the popular bluegrass standard, "Roll in My Sweet Baby's Arms." The banjo accompaniment makes use of many of the previous pedaling licks.

"Roll in My Sweet Baby's Arms"—in G

Track 32

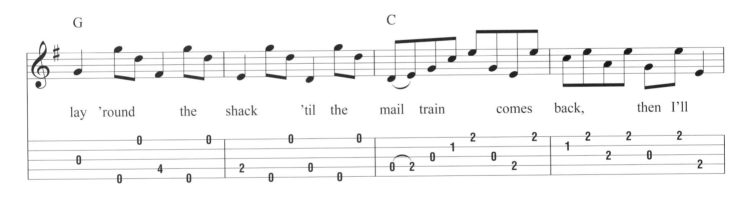

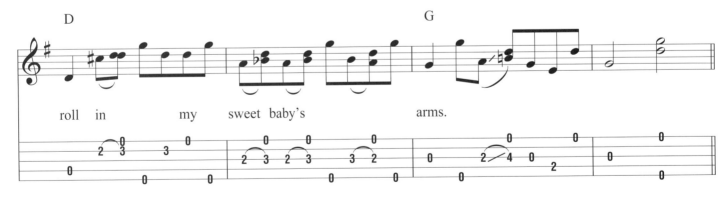

Pedaling Licks Up the Neck

Pedaling licks can also be played up the neck, using the moveable F, D, and barre formations:

 Pedaling D Formation Licks
Track 33

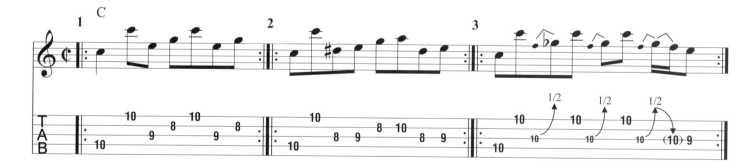

 Pedaling F Formation Licks
Track 34

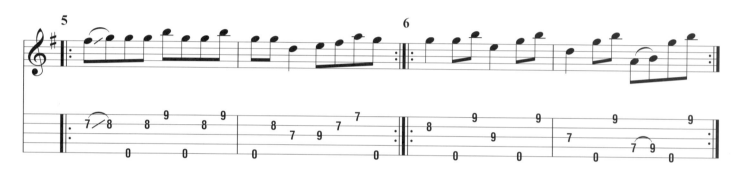

Notice in the last example that the fifth string is fretted in the C6 and C7 licks. There are two ways to finger these chords:

- Reach over the fretboard with your thumb to fret the fifth string, or…
- Fret the fifth string with your index finger and use the fingering of the second grid, below:

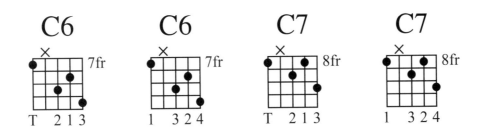

The last lick in Track 34 is usually played on a 5 chord that leads to a 1 chord (in this case, a D leading to a G). In the second bar of the lick, you slide up from an F formation to an Am formation, creating a bluesy D augmented chord with a suspended 4th. I bet you didn't know there are jazz chords in bluegrass! *(A major chord has three notes: the first, third, and fifth notes of the major scale. For example, C major is C, E, and G, the first, third, and fifth notes in the C major scale. An augmented chord has a sharp 5th [C augmented = C, E, and G#] and a suspended chord has a sharp 3rd [C, F, and G]).*

Pedaling Barre Licks

The next two licks are usually played during a pause in the vocal line. The first one is a Scruggs-ism that he often played on a 5 chord. It spans three formations of a D chord. The second lick, which includes some string stretching (bending), is one that Ralph Stanley played as a fill-in lick in the classic "How Mountain Girls Can Love." Since he played it at the same point in each chorus, it became a signature lick for that tune. *Any fill that you use, including one you invent, can become a signature lick if you always play it at the same place in a song.*

Two Licks

Track 36

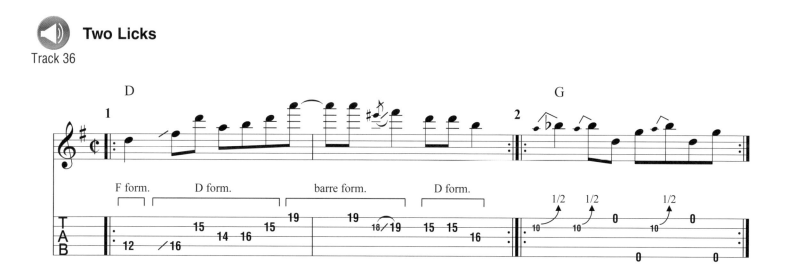

33

Here's the chorus of "Roll in My Sweet Baby's Arms" with up-the-neck accompaniment.

"Roll in My Sweet Baby's Arms"—in G (Up the Neck)

Track 37

Most of the up-the-neck pedaling licks in this section are moveable, even the ones that include an open fifth string. That means you can play them in any key. For example, tune your fifth string up to B, and play Track 38, an accompaniment to "Nine Pound Hammer" in the key of E.

"Nine Pound Hammer"—in E

Chop Chords

Chop chords are those percussive, staccato chord stabs, usually played on the **off-beats** (the second and fourth beats of a bar) when you want to simplify your picking and push the rhythm. They're often played during a chorus, or when the banjo player is singing. You create the staccato effect by lifting your fretting fingers after picking the chord, so that you're still touching the strings, but not pressing them down to the fretboard. This stops them from **sustaining** (ringing out).

When playing chop chords, some people pick the first and fourth strings with their middle finger and thumb. Others brush up on the top strings (first, second, and third) with their index or middle finger. The latter technique is used in Track 39, "Wreck of Old 97."

"Wreck of Old 97"—Chop Chords

Track 39

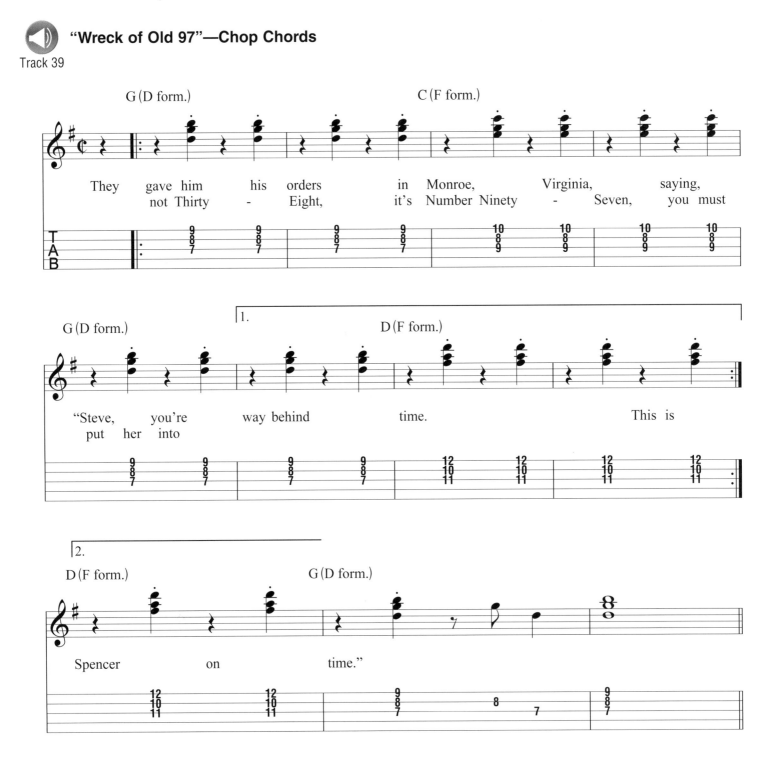

First- and Second-String Licks

It's amazing how many of the licks that are part of every bluegrass banjo player's repertoire came from Earl Scruggs' imagination—including most of the licks in this book. One backup technique he employed on tunes with moderate or slow tempos (yes, those do exist in bluegrass) uses just the first and second strings. The moveable barre and D formations are simplified.

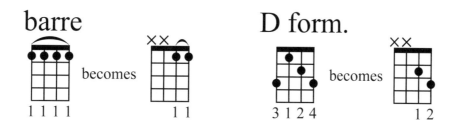

Notice the moveable chord relationships, pictured below:

- Wherever you play the simplified barre chord, the simplified D formation—played one fret higher—is the 4 chord. *Note that Roman numerals are used to indicate the 1, 4, and 5 chords in the following grids.*

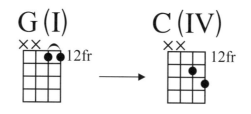

- That 4 chord, raised two frets, becomes the 5 chord:

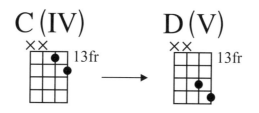

- Wherever you play the simplified barred chord, move it up three frets to play the dominant 7th version of that same chord (G becomes G7).

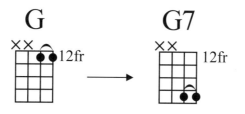

Here's a music theory tip about dominant 7th chords in bluegrass and most popular music: 7th chords are usually played when the progression moves up a 4th. For example, if you're going from G to C, play a G7; it leads to the C. It actually makes you want to hear the C!

- Wherever you play the simplified D formation, you can play a higher inversion of the same chord by playing the simplified barre chord *four frets higher*. (A chord's **inversion** contains a different arrangement of the same notes.)

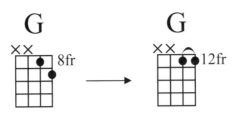

- When the simplified D formation is the I chord, lowering it two frets creates a dominant 9th chord, which is another version of a 7th chord.

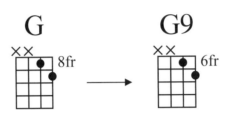

- If the simplified barre is the I chord, lower it two frets and it becomes the dominant 5 chord. For example:

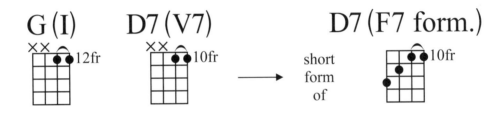

- When the simplified D formation is the I chord, the barre form—one fret lower—is the 5 chord.

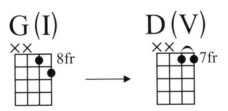

Here are some of the licks that are played with these formations:

First- and Second-String Licks

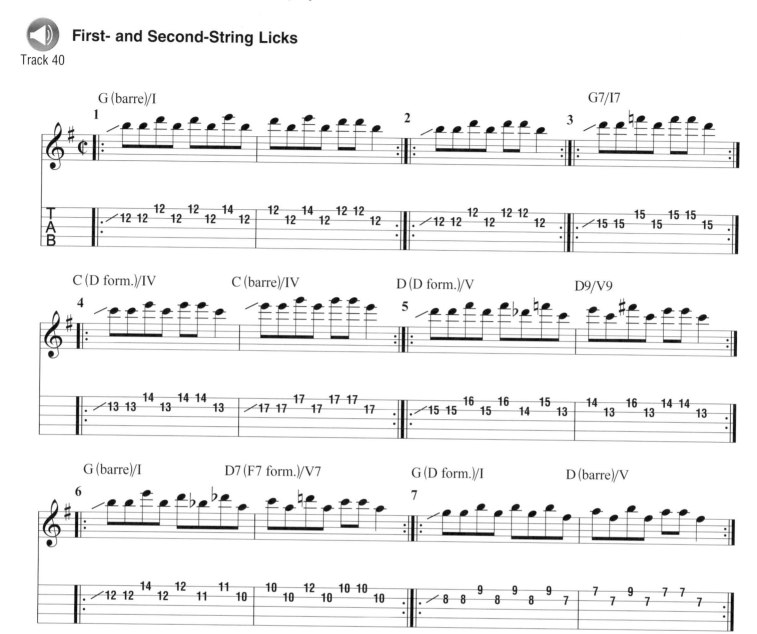

Here's an example of how to use the first- and second-string licks. The tune is a bluegrass standard: "Banks of the Ohio."

"Banks of the Ohio" (with First- and Second-String Licks)

Ending Licks

Here are several classic licks that end a song. Each lick is played in context, ending a final chorus of "Bury Me Beneath the Willow." Feel free to make up your own endings by varying these.

Key of G Endings

Track 42

Some of these key of G endings are in open position and some are played up the neck.

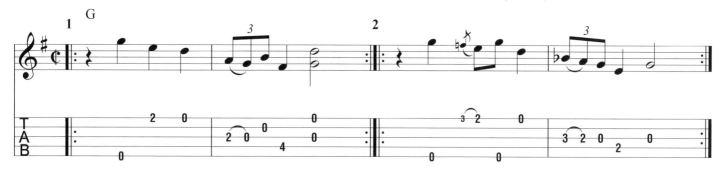

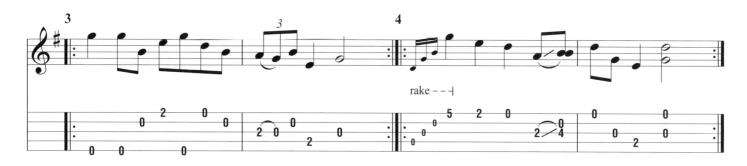

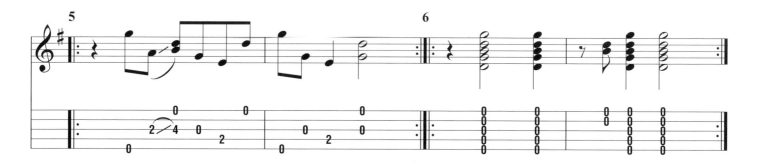

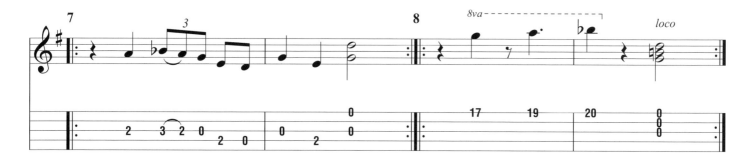

(Am form.)

(Am form.)   (Am form.)

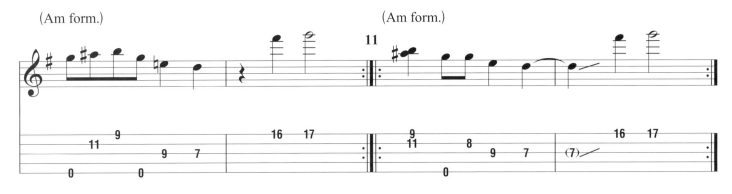

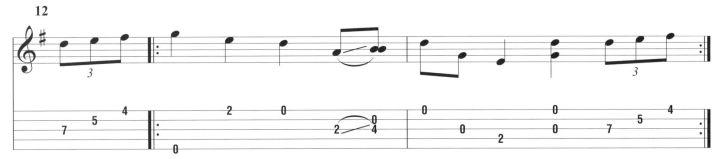

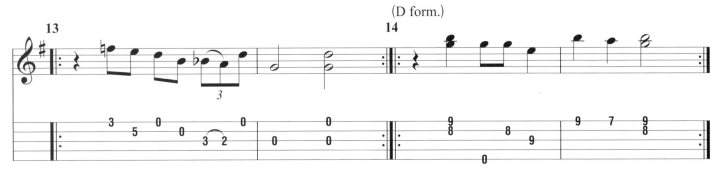

(D form.)

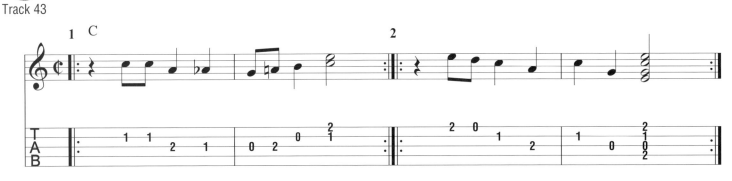

Key of C Endings

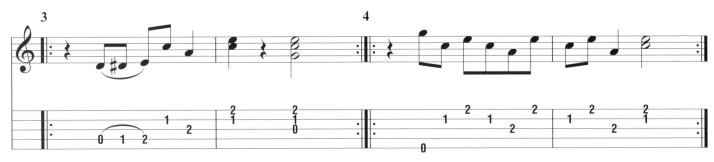

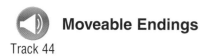
These ending licks are in the key of D, but they could be played in any key because they are based on moveable formations and don't include any open strings.

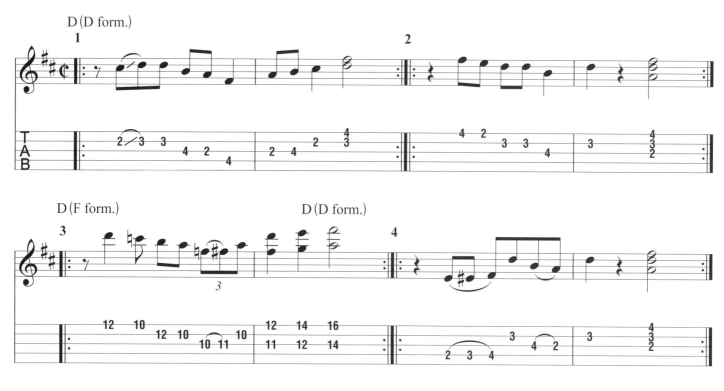

3/4 Time

When songs are played in **3/4 time** (three beats per measure instead of four or two; also called "three-quarter time" or "waltz time"), all the licks in this chapter must be adapted to that time signature. Here are some ways of doing that:

In and Out Roll and Variations—3/4 Time

Track 45

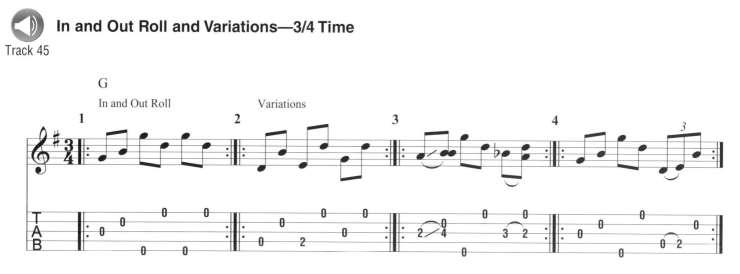

Forward Roll and Variations—3/4 Time

Track 46

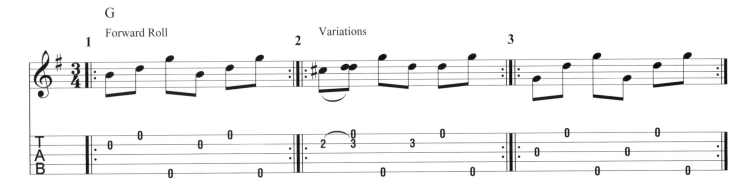

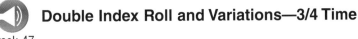

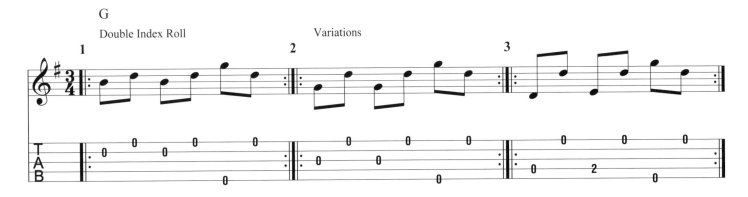

Double Index Roll and Variations—3/4 Time

Track 47

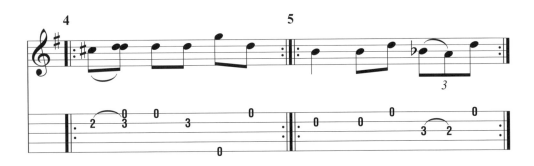

44

Backward Roll and Variations—3/4 Time

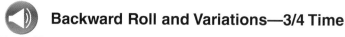

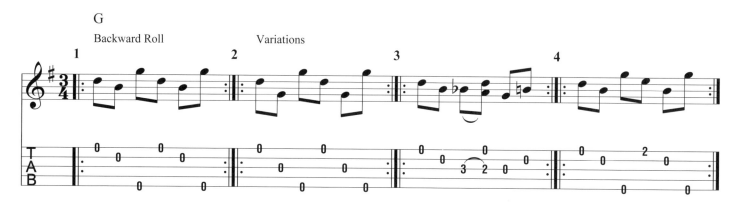

 Track 49

Forward/Backward Roll and Variations—3/4 Time

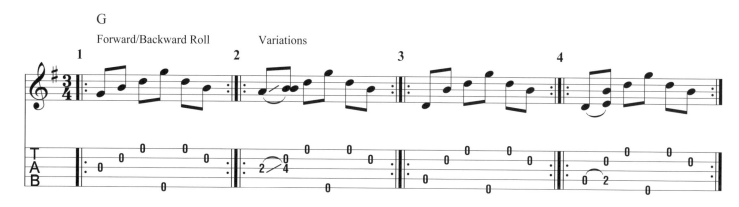

 Track 50

Double Backward Roll and Variations—3/4 Time

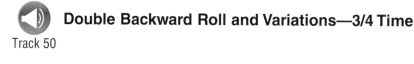

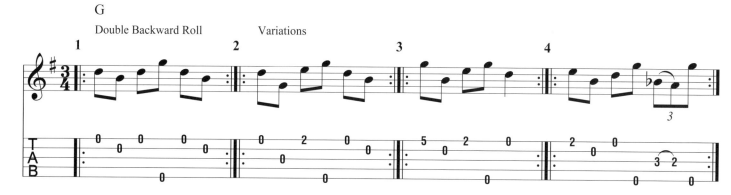

Tag Roll and Variations—3/4 Time

Track 51

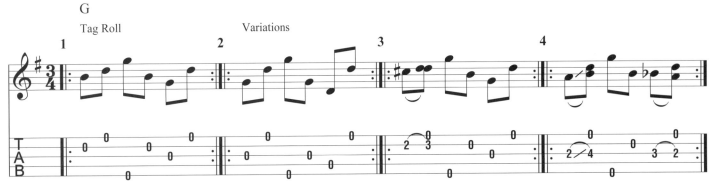

 Tag Endings—3/4 Time

Track 52

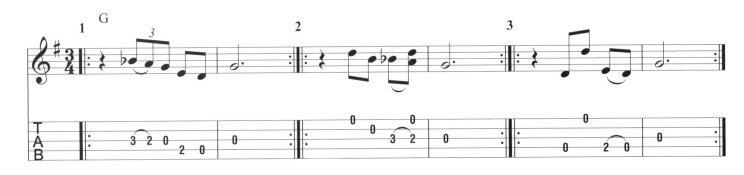

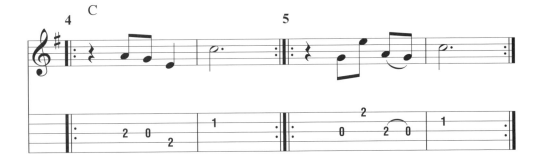

3/4 Time Connecting Licks

You can use the same connecting licks you learned in Tracks 18–21 for 3/4 time just by shortening them. Eliminate the first two eighth notes. For instance:

 Connecting Licks—3/4 Time

Track 53

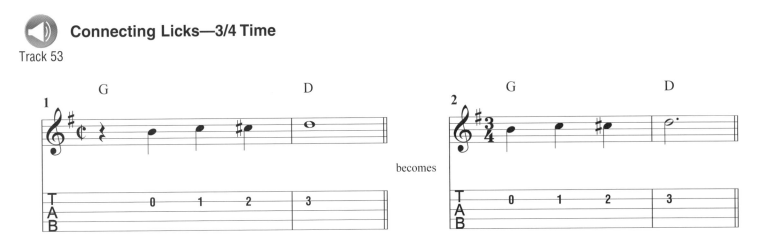

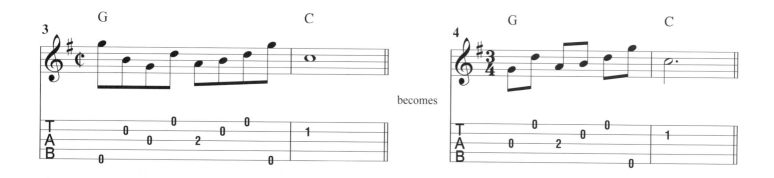

3/4 Time Pedaling Licks

You can adapt the pedaling licks you already learned to 3/4 time by eliminating the first two eighth notes:

Pedaling Licks—3/4 Time

Track 54

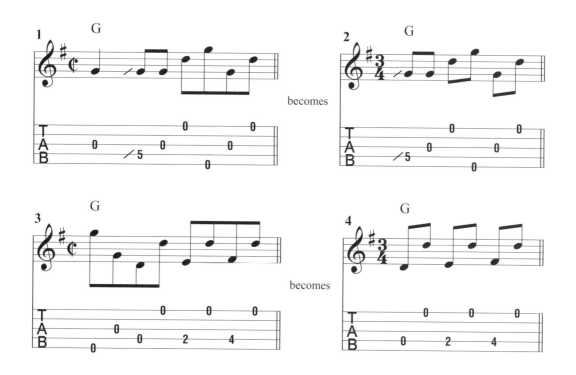

3/4 Time Chop Chords

In 3/4 time, chop chords fall on the second and third beat of each bar:

Chop Chords—3/4 Time

Track 55

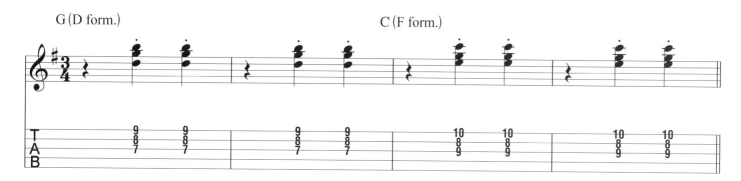

3/4 Time First- and Second-String Licks

Here are some sample first- and second-string licks in 3/4 time:

 First- and Second-String Licks—3/4 Time

Track 56

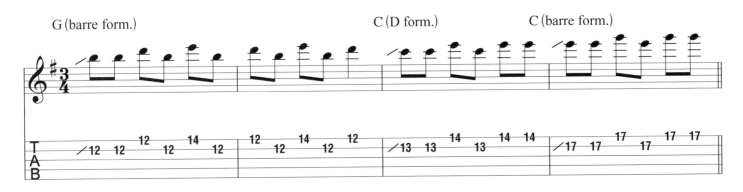

3/4 Time Ending Licks

The 3/4 time tag endings (Track 52) are good ending licks.

In Track 57, many of the previous 3/4 time licks are played to back up the old ballad "Beautiful Brown Eyes."

 "Beautiful Brown Eyes"—3/4 Time

Track 57

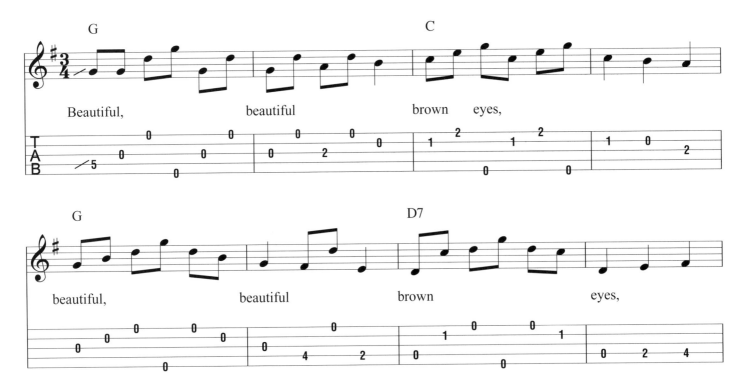

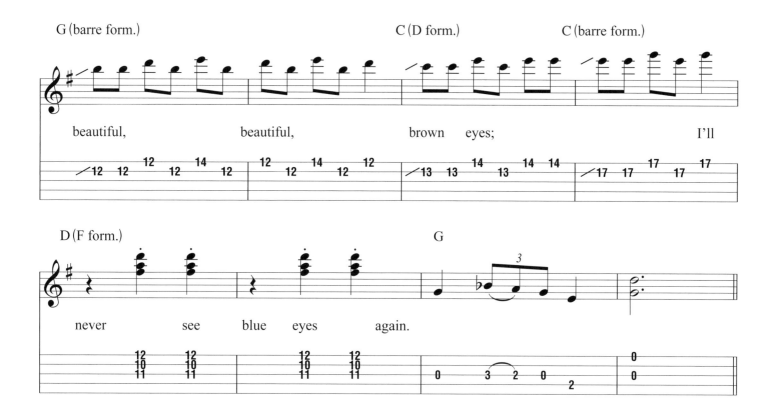

G (barre form.)   C (D form.)   C (barre form.)

beautiful,   beautiful,   brown eyes;   I'll

D (F form.)   G

never   see   blue   eyes   again.

SOLOING LICKS

Bluegrass banjoists have a vocabulary of licks, or bluegrass clichés, with which they embellish melodies. That's how they make any solo sound like a bluegrass banjo break!

Sliding Up to a Stressed Note

In any melody, some notes are stressed, or given more weight than others. This is sometimes called **accenting**, and applies to singing and to playing. To emphasize or accent a note, start a roll by sliding up to it from one or two frets back. Here are some examples:

 "Amazing Grace" (with Third- and Fourth-String Slides)

Track 58

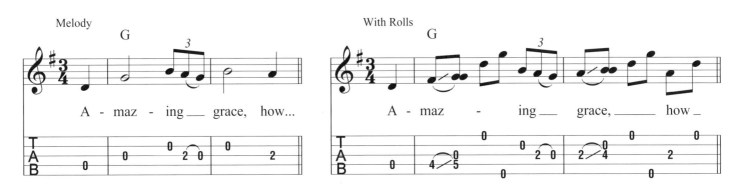

 "Wreck of Old 97" (with Second-String Slide)

Track 59

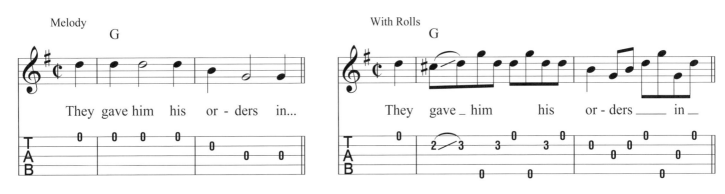

 "John Henry" (with First-String Slide)

Track 60

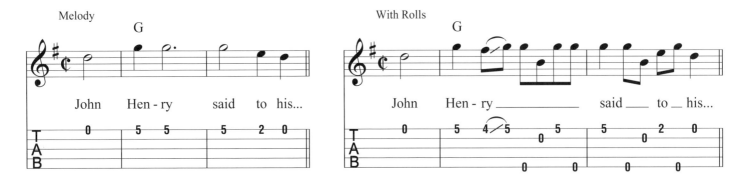

Hammer-On to a Stressed Note

Hammer-ons have the same effect as slides: they emphasize a note. (In fact, some of the previous samples could use hammer-ons instead of slides.) Here are some hammer-on examples:

"Bury Me Beneath the Willow" (with Fourth-String Hammer-On)

Track 61

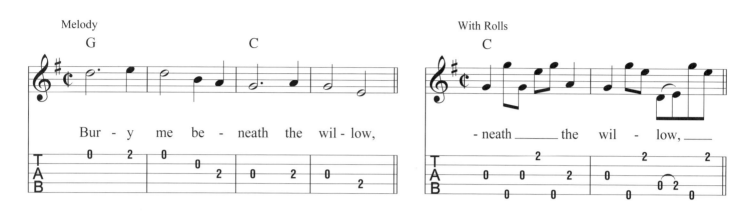

"Bury Me Beneath the Willow"—in C (with Third-String Hammer-On)

Track 62

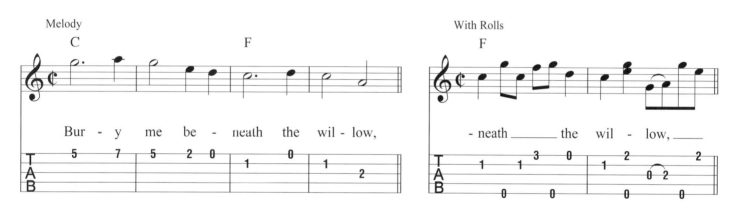

"Wreck of Old 97" (with Second-String Hammer-On)

Track 63

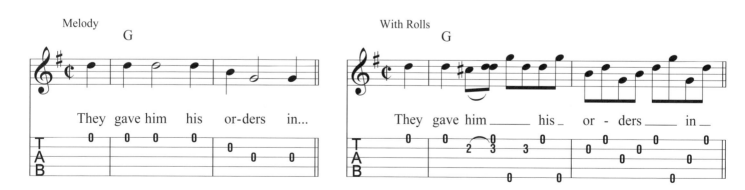

"Banks of the Ohio" (with First-String Hammer-On)

Track 64

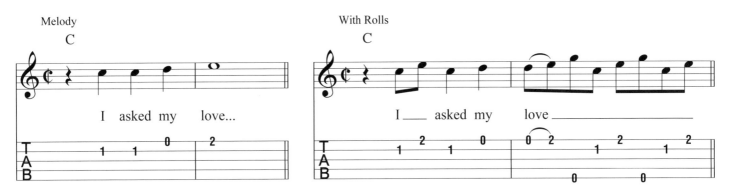

Pull-Offs

Pull-offs are yet another way to embellish melodies. Sometimes they include "blue notes" (flatted 3rds, 7ths, or 5ths that lend a bluesy flavor).

"Nine Pound Hammer" (with Fourth-String Pull-Off)

Track 65

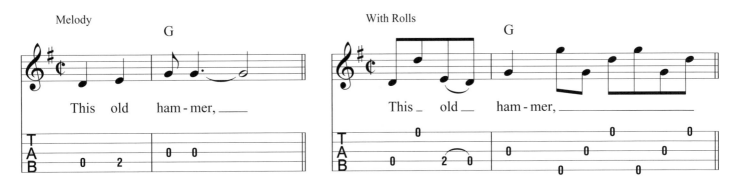

"Will the Circle Be Unbroken" (with Third-String Pull-Off)

Track 66

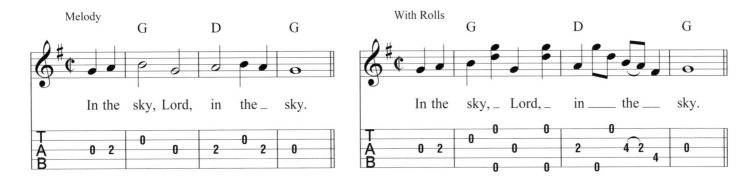

"Wreck of Old 97" (with Third-String Pull-Off and Blue Note)

Track 67

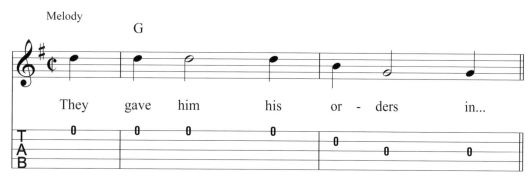

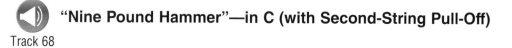

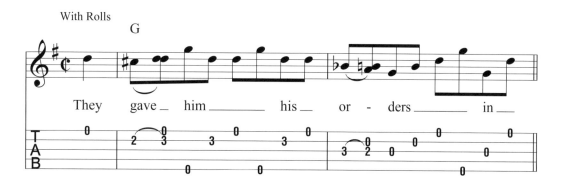

"Nine Pound Hammer"—in C (with Second-String Pull-Off)

Track 68

53

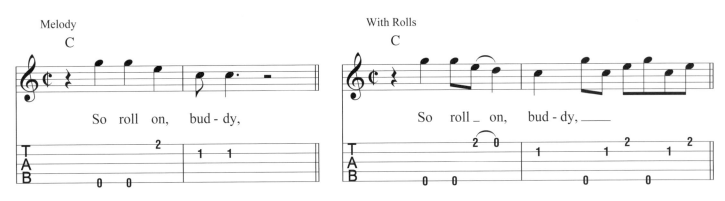

"Nine Pound Hammer"—in C (with First-String Pull-Off)

Track 69

Intros to Melodies That Have Pickup Notes

Some songs have a melody that begins a few notes prior to the downbeat, so they have a built-in introduction (think "Wildwood Flower," "When the Saints Go Marching In," or "Will the Circle Be Unbroken"). Those introductory notes kick off a solo, whether the banjo starts a tune or starts a solo within the tune. You can play the bare melody, or embellish it slightly:

"When the Saints Go Marching In"—Intro

Track 70

"Will the Circle Be Unbroken"—Intro

Track 71

"Wildwood Flower"—Intro

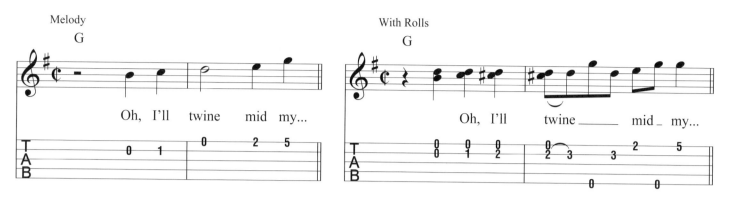

Intros in G

The rest of the intros (on the following pages) illustrate how to kick off a solo when the melody starts on the downbeat.

"Wabash Cannonball" (Melody Starts on Low D/Open Fourth String)

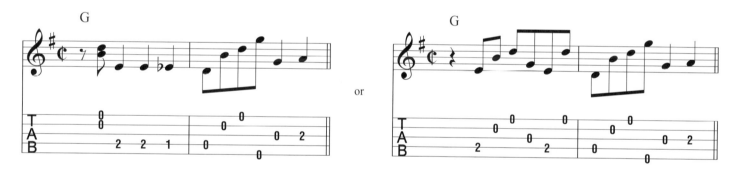

"This Train" (Melody Starts on G/Open Third String)

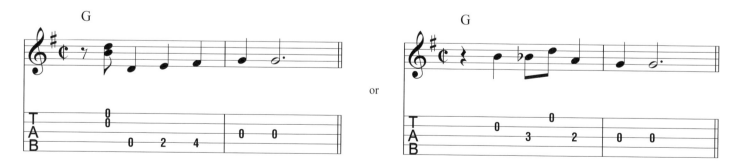

"Roll in My Sweet Baby's Arms" (Melody Starts on B/Open Second String)

Track 75

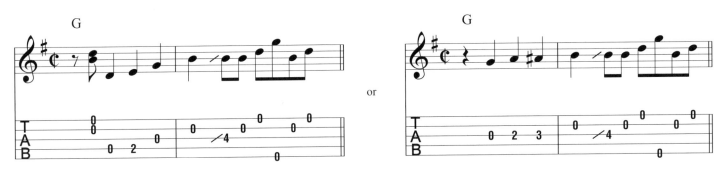

or

"Bury Me Beneath the Willow" (Melody Starts on D/Open First String)

Track 76

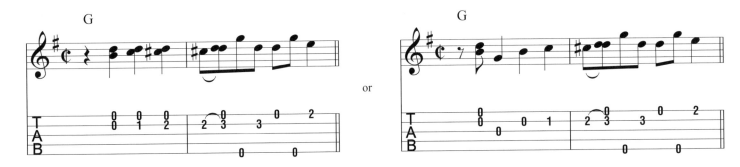

or

Intros in C

"Wabash Cannonball"—in C (Melody Starts on G/Open Third String)

Track 77

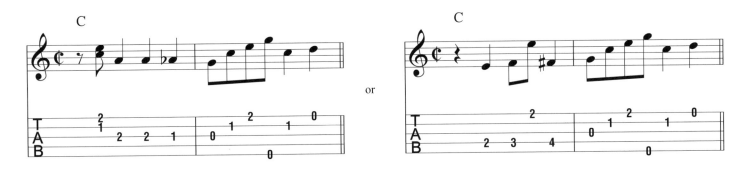

or

"This Train"—in C (Melody Starts on Second String)

Track 78

"Roll in My Sweet Baby's Arms"—in C (Melody Starts on First String)

Track 79

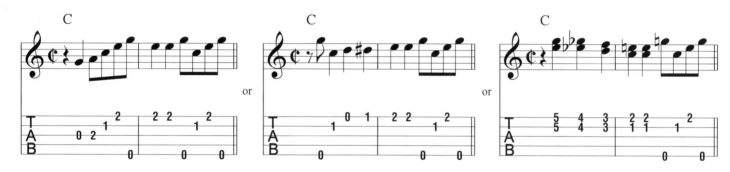

"Bury Me Beneath the Willow"—in C (Melody Starts on High G/First String)

Track 80

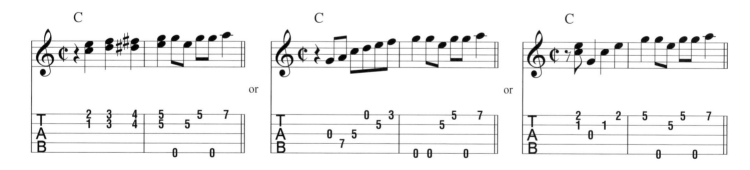

Moveable Intros

Each of the following intros is based on one of the moveable formations: the barre, D, or F formation.

D Formation Intros

🔊 **"Bury Me Beneath the Willow"** (Melody Starts on First String at the Barre)

Track 81

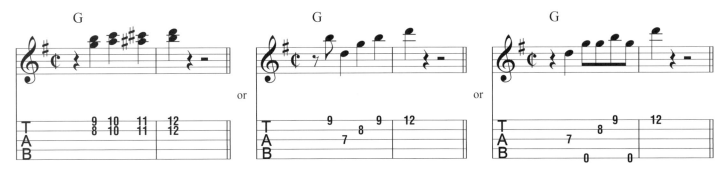

🔊 **"Roll in My Sweet Baby's Arms"** (Melody Starts on First String)

Track 82

🔊 **"This Train"** (Melody Starts on Second String)

Track 83

🔊 **"Wabash Cannonball"** (Melody Starts on Third String)

Track 84

Barre Formation Intros

Track 85

"Bury Me Beneath the Willow" (Melody Starts on First String)

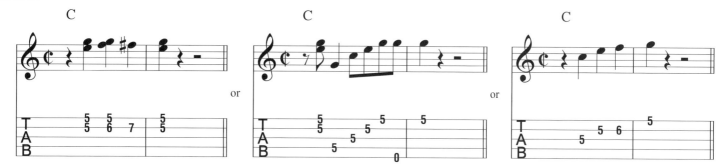

Track 86

"Roll in My Sweet Baby's Arms" (Melody Starts on Second String)

Track 87

"This Train" (Melody Starts on Third String)

F Formation Intros

Track 88

"This Train" (Melody Starts on First String)

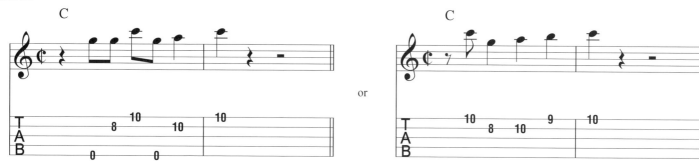

59

"Bury Me Beneath the Willow" (Melody Starts on Second String)

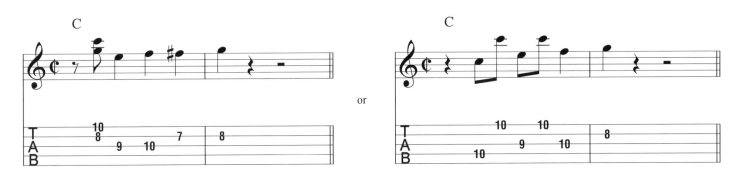

or

"Roll in My Sweet Baby's Arms" (Melody Starts on Third String)

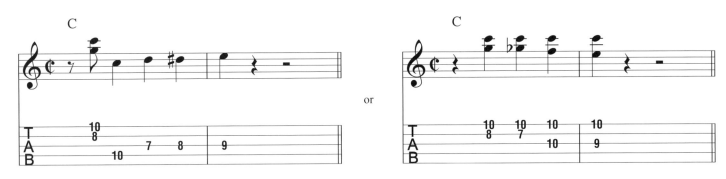

or

Using Bluegrass Clichés to Vary a Melody

Bluegrass banjo solos are often based on a song's melody. Because of the nature of Scruggs-style picking, the melody is surrounded by other notes as well (the notes that result from playing the melody within three-finger rolls). In spite of all these "extra" notes, the melody of the song can come through loud and clear.

Of course, some soloists totally ignore the melody and ad-lib "instant compositions" that fit the chord progression. But even when playing the melody, soloists can have some fun with it and add melodic embellishments with slides, hammer-ons, and pull-offs, as you've seen at the beginning of this chapter. These variations make a banjo break interesting.

In a typical banjo solo, you'll hear some of the song's melody, and you'll also hear moments where the melody disappears and bluegrass banjo clichés are inserted. Many of these licks come from Scruggs, of course! Look at some of these clichés and see how they're used in typical musical passages. You'll use the tunes you've already been studying as examples.

G Licks in Open Position

At the beginning of "Roll in My Sweet Baby's Arms," here's the basic melody, followed by an example of how to play it with rolls, then some "banjo cliché" variations:

"Roll in My Sweet Baby's Arms" (Licks for Two Bars of G)

Track 91

Like all the examples that follow, this variation can be used in countless songs, because so many tunes include a similar melodic phrase.

The next part of the melody to "Roll in My Sweet Baby's Arms" ends on a sustained A note on a D chord. After the melody note, the D chord lasts two bars, and there are several typical ways to fill those two bars of D, such as:

"Roll in My Sweet Baby's Arms" (Licks for Two Bars of D)

Track 92

The previous licks can also be used when there are melody notes in the two bars of D, instead of a sustained note. So could these "two bars of D" clichés:

G Licks Up the Neck

The second and third licks below are moveable; they're playable in any key.

"Roll in My Sweet Baby's Arms" (Up-the-Neck Licks for Two Bars of D)

Track 93

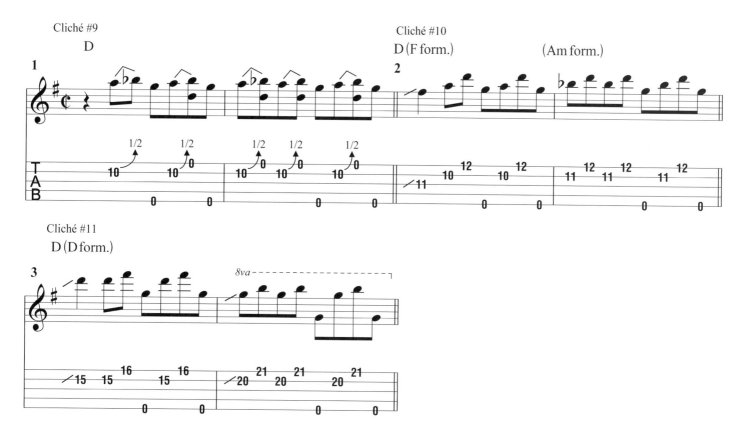

If there's only one bar of D (the 5 chord), as in "Nine Pound Hammer," there's a similar, shorter fill:

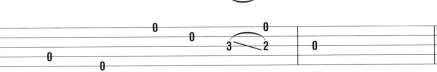 **"Nine Pound Hammer"** (Licks for One Bar of D)

Track 94

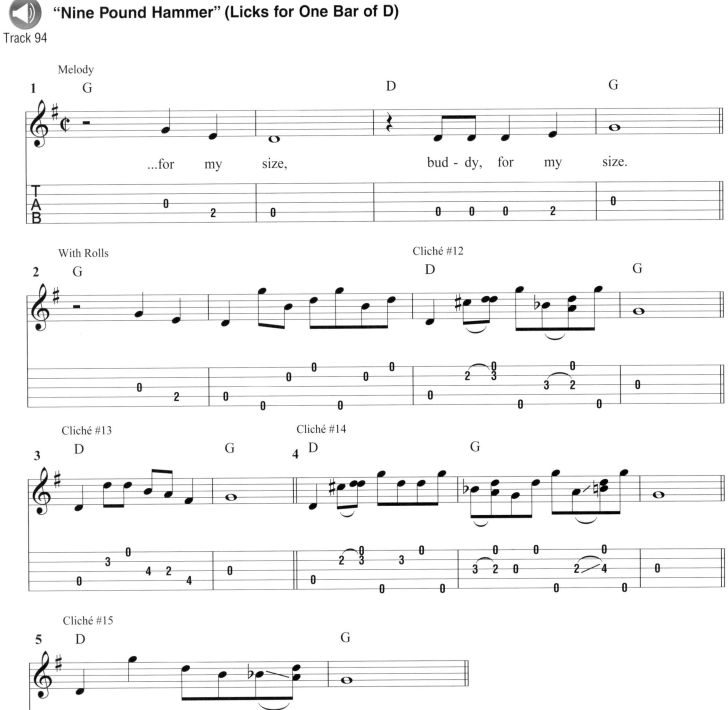

Moveable G Licks Based on the Am Formation

The moveable Am formation is a springboard for many up-the-neck clichés. Here's how it could be used in the first part of the chorus of "Roll in My Sweet Baby's Arms."

"Roll in My Sweet Baby's Arms" (Am Formation Licks)

Track 95

Perhaps you recognize some of these soloing clichés; they're shown in the Accompaniment section as "tag endings" or "pedaling licks." A number of them can be played in solos:

- The G tag endings in Track 12 can be used as one-bar D licks (like the previous Track 94 licks) if you start them with an open D/fourth string instead of a rest.

- The 10th and 11th licks in Track 29 can be played for two bars of D in a solo in the key of G, if you start them with an open D/fourth string instead of the open G/third string.

- The D licks in Track 31 can be used in solos as well as in accompaniment. The same goes for the moveable licks in Tracks 33–36.

Melodic Licks

At the beginning of the 1960s, Bill Keith, Bobby Thompson, and a few other bluegrass banjoists began incorporating scalar licks into their three-finger picking. They developed a style, often called **melodic picking** (or "Keith picking"), that enabled three-finger pickers to play fiddle tunes or scale-based licks as smoothly and rapidly as Scruggs licks. Most contemporary players use some melodic phrases, which are based on these scale licks.

(Notice the chord grids in the following music/tablature licks. They are not chords; they are fretting positions. In most of the licks, certain strings are played when fretted, then played unfretted. This is indicated by putting some of the dots on the grids in parentheses.)

Melodic G Licks

Track 96

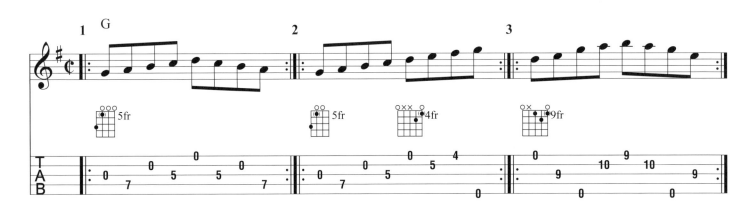

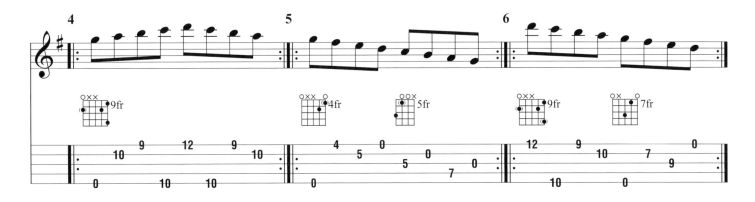

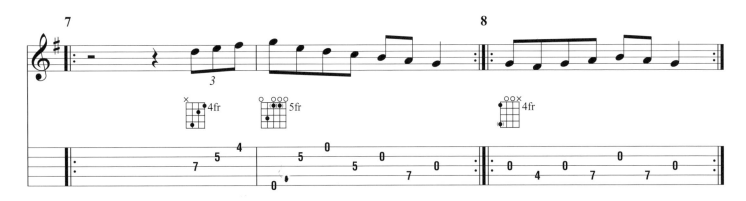

66

The fifth string is fretted in some of the previous licks. Some people reach around the neck with their thumb to fret it, but the fifth string can also be fretted with a finger:

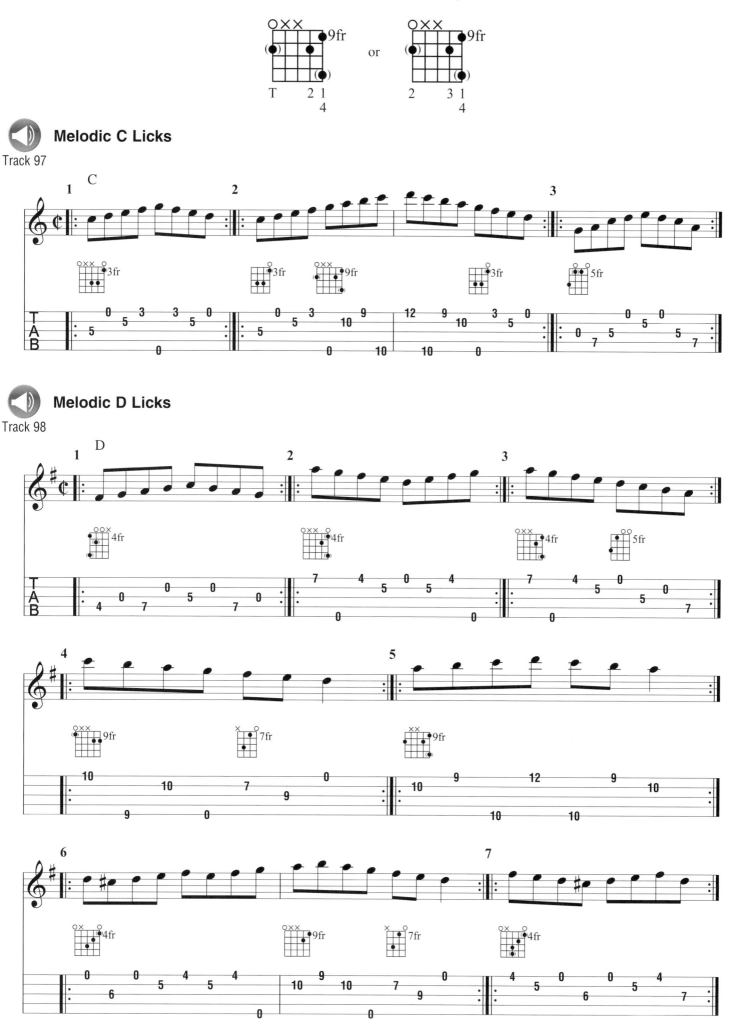

Melodic C Licks
Track 97

Melodic D Licks
Track 98

To become familiar with the melodic scales and finger positions, repeat the following exercise over and over:

Melodic Exercise

Track 99

Some fiddle tunes or melodic phrases that are impossible to duplicate note-for-note with Scruggs licks can be played with melodic licks. For example, here's the beginning of the famous fiddle tune, "Turkey in the Straw," and a way to play it melodic style.

"Turkey in the Straw" Intro

Track 100

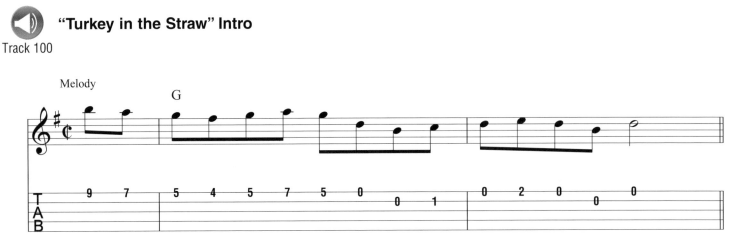

Melodic Style

Here's a solo to "Nine Pound Hammer" that uses melodic licks:

"Nine Pound Hammer"—Melodic Solo

Track 101

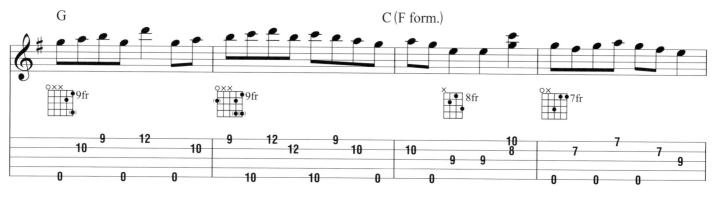

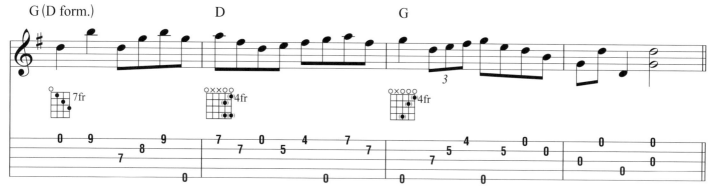

Some melodic licks incorporate blue notes (flatted 3rds, 5ths, and 7ths), which create a bluesy feel:

Bluesy Melodic Licks

Track 102

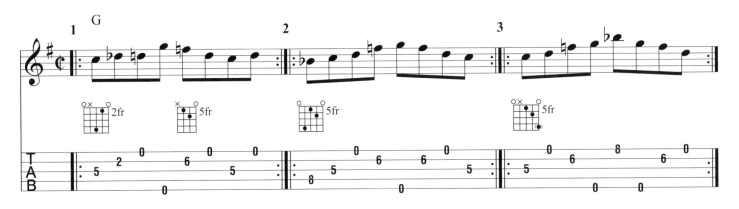

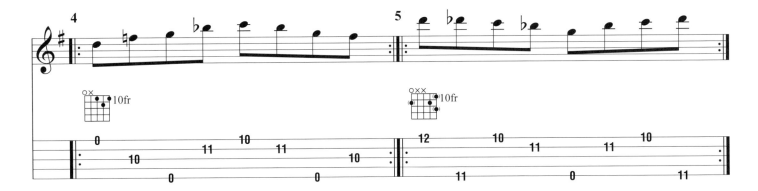

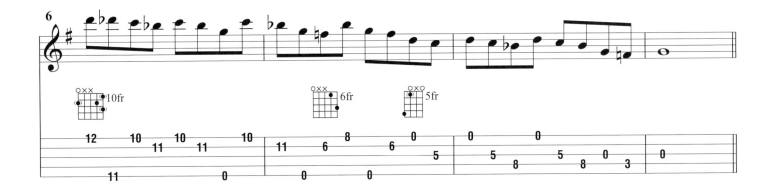

"Nine Pound Hammer"—Bluesy Melodic Solo

Track 103

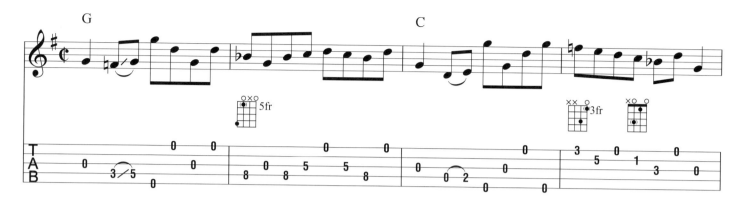

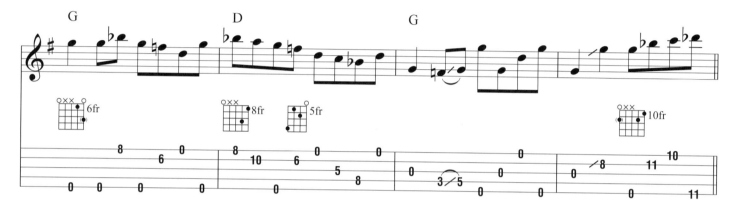

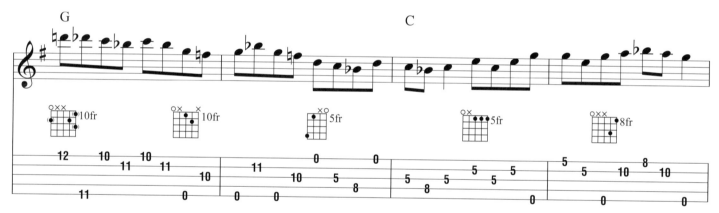

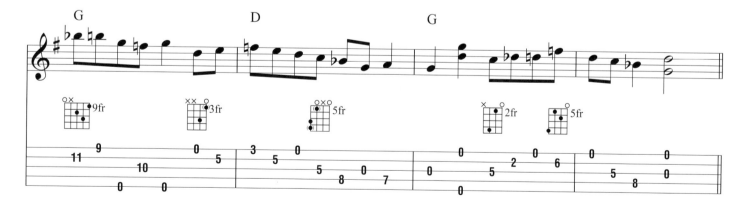

Triplets in Open Position

When a song has a slow or moderately slow tempo and most of the melody is played on the third and fourth strings, there's a triplet technique that is an interesting variation of Scruggs' style. Don Reno used it occasionally and it has been imitated by other banjo pickers. The melody is played with the thumb. Practice the following two bars, which contain the basic licks used in this style, then play the version of "Banks of the Ohio" that follows. It illustrates how to use the triplet licks to play a melody.

 Basic Triplet Licks

Track 104

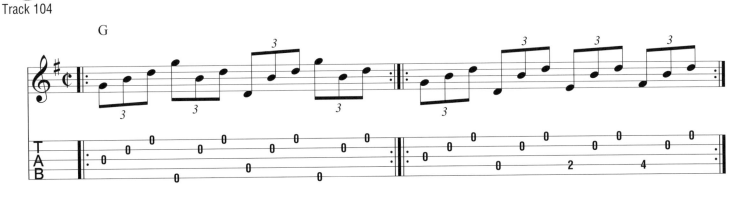

"Banks of the Ohio"

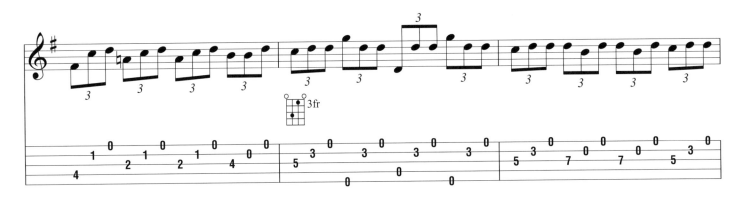

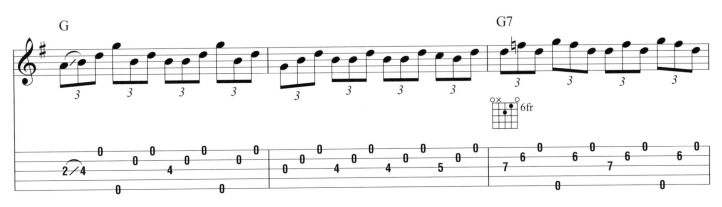

72

Triplets Up the Neck

A different triplet technique is sometimes used when playing a tune that has a moderate or slow tempo. It involves the use of moveable chords, up the neck. The melody is usually played on the first and second strings, so the basic triplet lick usually leads with the index or middle finger and is like the open-position triplet lick turned upside down! Practice the basic rolls on the next page, then play the version of "Banks of the Ohio" that follows.

Here are the moveable chord shapes used in this arrangement:

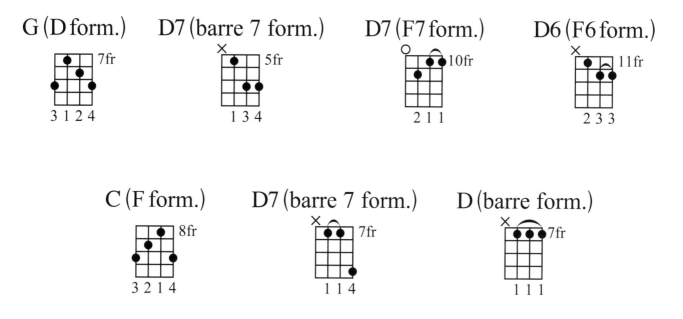

Basic Up-the-Neck Triplet Licks

Track 105

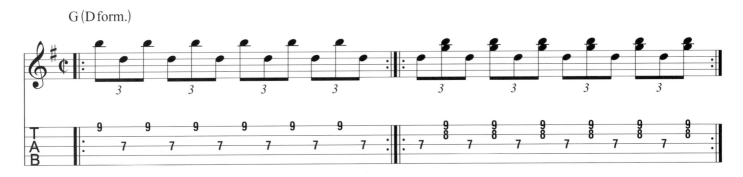

"Banks of the Ohio"

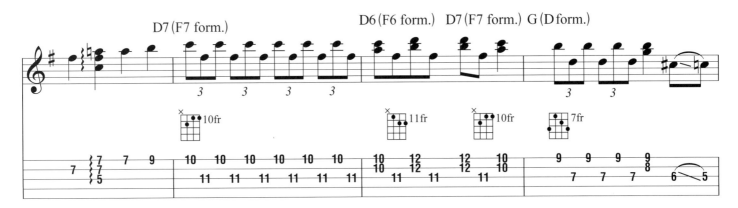

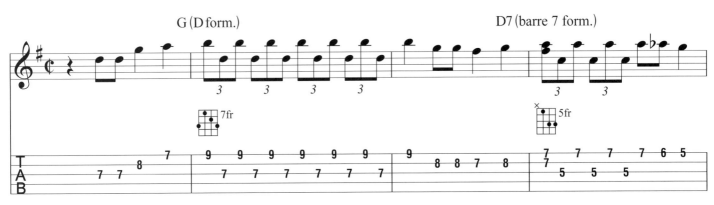

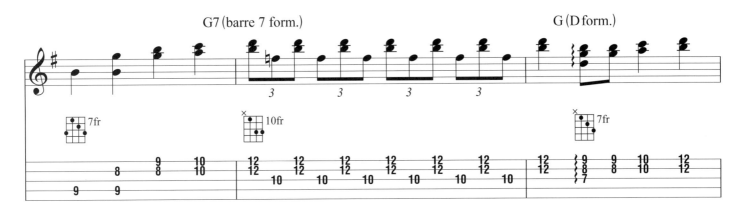

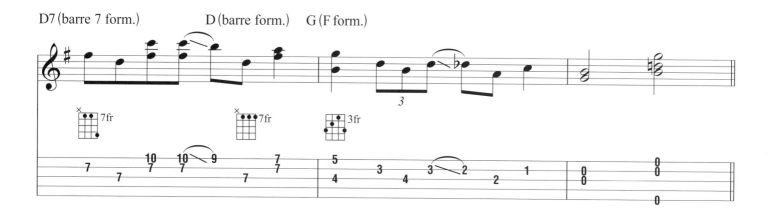

THE SONGS

The following tracks will help you become familiar with any of the tunes in this book that you don't already know. You can also use them as practice tracks, and play along with them. The banjo accompaniment makes use of many of the licks in the preceding pages.

The recordings include one verse and a chorus (if the song has one) for each song. Words for more verses are included here.

Track 106

"Amazing Grace"—Key of C

Chorus:
```
C              F      C                    G
Amazing grace, how sweet the sound that saved a wretch like me.
  C            F      C              G   C
I once was lost but now I'm found, was blind but now I see.
```

Verses:
'Twas grace that taught my eyes to see and grace my fears relieved.
How wondrous did that grace appear, the hour I first believed.

When we've been here ten thousand years, bright shining as the sun,
We've no less days to sing God's praise than when we first begun.

Track 107

"Banks of the Ohio"—Key of C

```
C                    G                          C
I asked my love to take a walk, take a walk, just a little walk,
                              F          C   G    C
Down beside where waters flow, down by the banks of the Ohio.
```

Chorus:
Then only say that you'll be mine, in no other arms entwine,
Down beside where waters flow, down by the banks of the Ohio.

Additional Verses:
I took her by her lily-white hand and led her down where the waters stand.
There I pushed her in to drown, and I watched her as she floated down.

I started home 'tween twelve and one; I cried "My God, what have I done?
I killed the only woman I loved, because she would not marry me."

"Beautiful Brown Eyes"—Key of D

Chorus:

D   G   D   A
Beautiful, beautiful brown eyes, beautiful, beautiful brown eyes,
D   G   A   D
Beautiful, beautiful brown eyes; I'll never see blue eyes again.

Verses:

I staggered into the bar room, I fell down on the floor.
And the very last words that I uttered: "I'll never get drunk anymore."

Oh Willie, my darling, I love you, I love you with all of my heart.
Tomorrow we were to be married, but liquor has kept us apart.

"Bury Me Beneath the Willow"—Key of C

C   F   C   G
My heart is sad and I am lonely for the only one I love.
     C   F   C   G   C
When will I see her, oh no, never, unless we meet in heaven above.

Chorus:

Bury me beneath the willow, under the weeping willow tree.
When she hears that I am sleeping, maybe then she'll think of me.

Additional Verses:

They told me that she did not love me, I could not believe it's true,
Until an angel softly whispered, "She no longer cares for you."

Tomorrow was to be our wedding. Lord, oh Lord, where can she be?
She's gone, she's gone to find another. She no longer cares for me.

"John Henry"—Key of C

C   G

When John Henry was a little baby, sittin' on his daddy's knee,

    C

He picked up a hammer and a little piece of steel, said,

                                                          G   C

"Hammer's gonna be the death of me, hammer's gonna be the death of me."

The captain said to John Henry, "I'm gonna bring that steam drill around.
I'm gonna bring that steam drill out on the job,
I'm gonna whup that steel on down, Lord, Lord, whup that steel on down."

Additional Verses:
John Henry told his captain "A man ain't nothing but a man,
But before I let your steam drill beat me down,
I'll die with a hammer in my hand, Lord, Lord, die with a hammer in my hand."

John Henry said to his shaker, "Shaker why don't you pray?
'Cause if I miss this little piece of steel,
Tomorrow be your burying day, Lord, Lord, tomorrow be your burying day."

John Henry hammered in the mountains. His hammer was striking fire,
And the last words I hear that poor boy say,
"Gimme a cool drink of water 'fore I die, Lord, Lord, cool drink of water 'fore I die."

John Henry, he drove fifteen feet, steam drill only made nine.
But he drove so hard that he broke his poor heart,
And he laid down his hammer and he died, Lord, Lord, laid down his hammer and he died.

So every Monday morning when the bluebirds begin to sing,
You can see John Henry out on the line.
You can hear John Henry's hammer ring, Lord, Lord, hear John Henry's hammer ring.

Track 111

"Little Birdie"—Key of G

G **D** **G**
Little birdie, little birdie, come and sing to me a song.
D **G**
I've a short while to be here, and a long time to be gone.

Verses:
Little birdie, little birdie, what makes your head so red?
After all that I been through, it's a wonder I ain't dead.

Little birdie, little birdie, what makes you fly so high?
It's because I am a true little bird and I do not fear to die.

Track 112

"Nine Pound Hammer"—Key of G

G **C** **G** **D** **G**
Nine pound hammer is a little too heavy for my size, buddy, for my size.

Chorus:
G **C** **G** **D** **G**
Roll on buddy, don'tcha roll so slow. How can I roll, when the wheel won't go?

Additional Verses:
I'm going on the mountain, for to see my baby,
And I ain't coming back, no I ain't coming back.
There ain't no hammer, down in this tunnel
That can ring like mine, that can ring like mine.

Rings like silver, and it shines like gold.
Rings like silver, and it shines like gold.

This old hammer, it killed John Henry.
Ain't gonna kill me, it ain't gonna kill me.

It's a long way to Harlan, and a long way to Hazard
Just to get a little brew, just to get a little brew.

"Roll in My Sweet Baby's Arms"—Key of G

```
G                                                        D
Ain't gonna work on the railroad, ain't gonna work on the farm.
G                              C
Lay around the shack 'til the mail train comes back,
           D                  G
Then I'll roll in my sweet baby's arms.
```

Chorus:
Roll in my sweet baby's arms, roll in my sweet baby's arms,
Lay around the shack 'til the mail train comes back,
Then I'll roll in my sweet baby's arms.

Additional Verses:
Where was you last Friday night while I was locked up in jail?
Walkin' the streets with another man, wouldn't even go my bail.

They tell me your parents do not like me, they have drove me away from your door.
If I had all my time to do over, I would never go there anymore.

Mama's a ginger cake baker, sister can weave and can spin.
Dad's got an interest in that old cotton mill, just watch that old money roll in.

"This Train"—Key of C

```
C                                                              G
This train is bound for glory, this train. This train is bound for glory, this train.
C                         F
This train is bound for glory. Don't take nothing but the righteous and the holy.
C        G          C
This train is bound for glory, this train.
```

This train don't carry no gamblers, this train. This train don't carry no gamblers, this train.
This train don't carry no gamblers, no hypocrites, no midnight ramblers.
This train is bound for glory, this train.

Additional Verses:
This train is built for speed now, this train. This train is built for speed now, this train.
This train is built for speed now, fastest train you ever did see.
This train is bound for glory, this train.

This train don't carry no liars, this train. This train don't carry no liars, this train.
This train don't carry no liars, no hypocrites and no high flyers.
This train is bound for glory, this train.

"Wabash Cannonball"—Key of G

G   C

From the great Atlantic Ocean to the wide Pacific shore,

            D   G

From the high and verdant mountains, past the southland by the shore,

                                         C

She's mighty tall and handsome and she's known quite well by all.

            D   G

She's a reg'lar combination on the Wabash Cannonball.

Chorus:
Now listen to the jingle and the rumble and the roar,
As she dashes through the woodlands, and speeds along the shore.
See the mighty rushing engines, hear the merry bell's clear call,
As you travel across the country on the Wabash Cannonball.

Additional Verses:
Oh, the Eastern states are dandy so the Western people say,
From New York to St. Louis and Chicago by the way.
Through the hills of Minnesota where the rippling waters fall,
No chances can be taken on the Wabash Cannonball.

Here's to Daddy Claxton, may his name forever stand,
And may he be remembered in the courts throughout our land.
When his earthly race is over and the curtain around him falls,
They'll carry him to glory on the Wabash Cannonball.

"When the Saints Go Marching In"—Key of E

Chorus:
E   B

Oh, when the saints go marching in, when the saints go marching in,

            E   A   E   B   E

Oh Lord, I want to be in that number, when the saints go marching in.

Verses:
And when the sun begins to shine, and when the sun begins to shine,
Oh Lord, I want to be in that number, when the saints go marching in.

Oh, when the trumpet sounds the call, oh, when the trumpet sounds the call,
Oh Lord, I want to be in that number, when the saints go marching in.

"Wildwood Flower"—Key of G

G   D   G

Oh, I'll twine mid my ringlets of raven black hair,

                                D   G

With the lilies so pale and the roses so fair,

                                   C   G

And the myrtle so bright with an emerald hue,

                              D   G

And the pale daisy with eyes of bright blue.

I'll dance, I'll sing and my laugh shall be gay.
I'll charm ev'ry heart, in this crowd I survey.
And I'll long to see him regret the dark hour
When he'd gone and neglected this pale wildwood flower.

Additional Verse:
He told me he loved me and promised to love,
Through ill and misfortune all others above.
Another has won him, ah misery to tell.
He left me in silence with no word of farewell.

"Will the Circle Be Unbroken"—Key of E

E   A   E

I was standing by the window on one cold and cloudy day,

                                                              B   E

And I saw the hearse come rolling for to carry my mother away.

Chorus:
Will the circle be unbroken by and by Lord, by and by?
There's a better home awaiting in the sky, Lord, in the sky.

Additional Verses:
Lord, I told the undertaker, "Undertaker please drive slow,
For this lady you are carrying, Lord, I hate to see her go."

Oh, I followed close behind her, tried to hold up and be brave.
But I could not hide my sorrow when they laid her in the grave.

I went back home, the home was lonesome since my mother, she was gone.
All my brothers and sisters crying, what a home so sad and alone.

"Wreck of Old 97"—Key of A

```
A                            D                         A                            E
```
They gave him his orders in Monroe, Virginia, saying "Steve, you're way behind time.
```
    A                        D                              A          E          A
```
This is not Thirty-Eight, it's number Ninety-Seven. You must put her into Spencer on time."

Additional Verses:
Steve turned around to his black and greasy fireman, saying "Shovel on a little more coal.
And when we reach that grade into Danville, just watch old Ninety-Seven roll."

It's a long, hard road from Lynchburg to Danville and it's lined with a three-mile grade.
It was on that road that he lost his airbrakes, you see what a jump he made.

They were going down the track, ninety miles an hour, when his whistle broke into a scream.
He was found in the wreck with his hand on the throttle, scalded to death by the steam.

Now all you women, please take warning from this day on and learn,
Never speak harsh words to your kind and loving husband,
He may leave you and never return.

LISTENING SUGGESTIONS

Every bluegrass banjo picker should hear Bill Monroe's late 1940s sessions, when Lester Flatt and Earl Scruggs were in the band. This was the band that defined the bluegrass sound.

The 1950s are considered by many to be the golden age of bluegrass. The recordings from the '50s by Flatt and Scruggs, Bill Monroe, Reno and Smiley, and the Stanley Brothers are essential listening. Jimmy Martin (with J.D. Crowe on banjo) is classic '50s bluegrass, as are Mac Wiseman, the Osborne Brothers, and the Lonesome Pine Fiddlers. In the early 1960s, the Country Gentlemen (Eddie Adcock on banjo) and Jim and Jesse McReynolds (with Allen Shelton on banjo) are important.

The 1960s saw innovations like "newgrass" (experimental bluegrass that incorporated elements of rock, jazz, country, and extended jams) and melodic picking—an adjunct to Scruggs' style based on scalar licks that enabled one to play note-for-note fiddle tunes and scale-based solos. Important players include Bill Keith, Tony Trischka, John Hartford, Bill Emerson, Alan Munde, Bobby Thompson, Pete Wernick, and Doug Dillard.

More recent bluegrass banjo players of note include Béla Fleck, Alison Brown, Scott Vestal, Jim Mills (with Ricky Skaggs), Noam Pikelny, and Jens Kruger. Many of these pickers are pushing the envelope… daring to go where no bluegrass banjo has gone before. Contemporary bluegrass bands that feature excellent banjoists include Alison Krauss and Union Station, the Nashville Bluegrass Band, Punch Brothers, Laurie Lewis, and Del McCoury Band… to name just a few.

WHERE TO GO FROM HERE

Bluegrass is like a language, and licks are like words or phrases. Knowing how to play the licks is part of learning the language (vocabulary); learning how to string them together and play them in a context that makes sense is like grammar and sentence structure. That's why listening to the players mentioned above is so important. A dictionary helps you learn a language, but listening to native speakers and copying them is just as essential.

The next step is playing with other people; it's like having conversations with those who speak the language. Every banjo player needs to find a guitar playing friend—hopefully one who enjoys singing and will put up with your first attempts at having a bluegrass conversation. Once you've practiced the licks in this collection, grab every opportunity to play with other people and try out the banjo "words and phrases" you've learned here. There are few things as rewarding as playing music with other people, so don't be shy. Get out there and pick!

ABOUT THE AUTHOR

Fred Sokolow is best known as the author of over 150 instructional and transcription books and DVDs for guitar, banjo, Dobro, lap steel, mandolin, and ukulele. Fred has long been a well-known West Coast multi-string performer and recording artist, particularly on the acoustic music scene. The diverse musical genres covered in his books and DVDs, along with several bluegrass, jazz, and rock CDs he has released, demonstrate his mastery of many musical styles. Whether he's playing Delta bottleneck blues, bluegrass or old-time banjo, '30s swing guitar or screaming rock solos, he does it with authenticity and passion.

Fred's other banjo books include:

- *Fretboard Roadmaps • 5-String Banjo*, book/audio, Hal Leonard

- *The Complete Bluegrass Banjo Method*, book/audio, Hal Leonard

- *The Beatles for Banjo*, book, Hal Leonard

- *101 Five-String Banjo Tips*, book/CD, Hal Leonard

- *Hal Leonard Tenor Banjo Method*, book/audio, Hal Leonard

- *Blues Banjo*, book/audio, Hal Leonard

Email Fred with any questions about these or his other banjo (guitar, uke, mandolin) books at: Sokolowmusic.com.

Hal Leonard Banjo Play-Along Series

Hal•Leonard® BANJO PLAY-ALONG

AUDIO ACCESS INCLUDED

INCLUDES TAB

The Banjo Play-Along Series will help you play your favorite songs quickly and easily with incredible backing tracks to help you sound like a bona fide pro! Just follow the banjo tab, listen to the demo track on the CD or online audio to hear how the banjo should sound, and then play along with the separate backing tracks. The CD is playable on any CD player and also is enhanced so Mac and PC users can adjust the recording to any tempo without changing the pitch! Books with online audio also include PLAYBACK+ options such as looping and tempo adjustments. Each Banjo Play-Along pack features eight cream of the crop songs.

1. BLUEGRASS
Ashland Breakdown • Deputy Dalton • Dixie Breakdown • Hickory Hollow • I Wish You Knew • I Wonder Where You Are Tonight • Love and Wealth • Salt Creek.
00102585 Book/CD Pack..........................$14.99

2. COUNTRY
East Bound and Down • Flowers on the Wall • Gentle on My Mind • Highway 40 Blues • If You've Got the Money (I've Got the Time) • Just Because • Take It Easy • You Are My Sunshine.
00105278 Book/CD Pack..........................$14.99

3. FOLK/ROCK HITS
Ain't It Enough • The Cave • Forget the Flowers • Ho Hey • Little Lion Man • Live and Die • Switzerland • Wagon Wheel.
00119867 Book/CD Pack..........................$14.99

4. OLD-TIME CHRISTMAS
Away in a Manger • Hark! the Herald Angels Sing • Jingle Bells • Joy to the World • O Holy Night • O Little Town of Bethlehem • Silent Night • We Wish You a Merry Christmas.
00119889 Book/CD Pack..........................$14.99

5. PETE SEEGER
Blue Skies • Get up and Go • If I Had a Hammer (The Hammer Song) • Kisses Sweeter Than Wine • Mbube (Wimoweh) • Sailing Down My Golden River • Turn! Turn! Turn! (To Everything There Is a Season) • We Shall Overcome.
00129699 Book/CD Pack..........................$17.99

6. SONGS FOR BEGINNERS
Bill Cheatham • Black Mountain Rag • Cripple Creek • Grandfather's Clock • John Hardy • Nine Pound Hammer • Old Joe Clark • Will the Circle Be Unbroken.
00139751 Book/CD Pack..........................$14.99

7. BLUEGRASS GOSPEL
Cryin' Holy unto the Lord • How Great Thou Art • I Saw the Light • I'll Fly Away • I'll Have a New Life • Man in the Middle • Turn Your Radio On • Wicked Path of Sin.
00147594 Book/Online Audio $14.99

8. CELTIC BLUEGRASS
Billy in the Low Ground • Cluck Old Hen • Devil's Dream • Fisher's Hornpipe • Little Maggie • Over the Waterfall • The Red Haired Boy • Soldier's Joy.
00160077 Book/Online Audio $14.99

HAL•LEONARD®
www.halleonard.com